PASTA
PRESTO

100
Fast & Fabulous Pasta Sauces

N O R M A N   K O L P A S

CB
CONTEMPORARY
BOOKS
CHICAGO · NEW YORK

Library of Congress Cataloging-in-Publication Data

Kolpas, Norman.
    Pasta presto : 100 fast and fabulous pasta sauces / Norman Kolpas.
       p.   cm.
    Includes index.
    ISBN 0-8092-4676-7 (pbk.) : $7.95
    1. Sauces.   2. Cookery (Macaroni)   I. Title.   II. Title: Pasta
sauces.
    TX819.A1K65   1988
    641.8′22—dc19   87-35555
                                                      CIP

Published by Contemporary Books, Inc.
180 North Michigan Avenue, Chicago, Illinois 60601
Manufactured in the United States of America
Library of Congress Catalog Card Number: 87-35555
International Standard Book Number: 0-8092-4511-6 (cloth)
                                      0-8092-4676-7 (paper)

Published simultaneously in Canada by Beaverbooks, Ltd.
195 Allstate Parkway, Valleywood Business Park
Markham, Ontario L3R 4T8 Canada

CONTENTS

ACKNOWLEDGMENTS

I am grateful to Hu Goldman, Peter Goldman, Chuck Stewart, Michael Gore, Evonne and Joseph Magee, Ann Katzen, and Nancy Brown for their enthusiasm as taste-testers of the recipes in this book. They sat through meals composed of several different pasta sauces, ate them cheerfully, and offered useful advice that has helped make this the best book it could possibly be.

Most of all, I want to thank my wife, Katie, who endured several months of dinners composed solely of pasta with sauces. She tasted virtually every recipe, and though she claimed to love them all, her critical insights and perseverance kept me creatively on track.

INTRODUCTION

Topped with a freshly made sauce, pasta is one of the quickest, most nutritious, most satisfying, and most economical main courses anyone can cook.

But the inspiration of most cooks begins to wane after they've cooked their standard tomato or marinara sauce, their usual meat sauce, and maybe a somewhat more adventurous clam sauce or pasta Alfredo-style. (Many don't even go beyond their favorite can or jar or one of the fresher sauces now available in many supermarket deli cases.) Sooner or later, cooks who love pasta want something different that's still easy and dependably delicious.

This book offers you something new and delicious a hundred times over. But it never does so at the sacrifice of convenience. Every sauce in this book can be cooked in about 30 minutes or less. All of the sauces are meant to top standard pastas that you can easily buy in any supermarket. (If you want to take the time to search for unusual or freshly made pastas, or to make pasta from scratch yourself, go ahead; you'll find a host of toppings here that will do them justice.) And virtually all of the recipes contain standard ingredients that most people ordinarily have on hand or that can be bought with little difficulty in good-sized towns or cities.

The book begins with the very basics of pasta sauce-making—a well-stocked pantry. First, of course, are the pastas. You'll find a list of some of the more common shapes, along with cooking instructions. Next comes a guide to some of the sauce and topping ingredients it would be wise to keep in stock.

The 100 recipes that follow the introductory section are grouped by their predominant ingredients, with separate chapters on sauces featuring seafood, poultry and meat sauces, sauces based primarily on vegetables, cream and cheese sauces, and simple sauces based on butter and oil. In some cases, I've made a judgment call on which section a recipe should appear in if it has several different kinds of ingredients: Browned Butter, Garlic, and Parmesan appears in the butter and oil chapter, even though it is seasoned with cheese; Spicy Cheddar with Bacon is grouped with the cream and cheese sauces, even though it includes bits of crisp bacon; and Creamy Parmesan Primavera, rich and creamy though it is, has such a wealth of vegetables in it that it has to be grouped with the vegetable sauces.

Since Italy is the land of pasta, many of the recipes are Italian in origin or inspiration. But sprinkled throughout the book you'll also find sauces and toppings with the flavors of China, France, Britain, Mexico, Hungary, the United States, and other countries.

Beyond this variety, I hope you'll find something else in the recipes: flexibility. Though I've created, written, or edited hundreds, maybe thousands, of recipes, when I do my day-to-day cooking at home I *never* follow recipes. Knowing the principles of cooking, I always improvise, relying on taste, touch, sight, smell, and even hearing to know when something is cooking properly, when it works. That is why, in every recipe in this book, I give not only a time range for the various stages of preparation, but also all kinds of sensory cues for you to know when something is done, when it's ready. I hope that, once you've tried and mastered a particular recipe, you'll have the confidence to start playing with it, changing and adding ingredients and methods to suit your taste. Please, make this book your own.

A GUIDE TO PASTA

Enter any supermarket nowadays and you're likely to be confronted by a bewildering array of pastas. There are all kinds of strands and ribbons; tubes short and long, fat and thin; tiny shells and huge shells; and a variety of unusual shapes, from spirals to bow ties to wagon wheels to any number of imaginative creations.

Now you can find many of them fresh as well as dried. And the colors: pastas colored green with spinach or parsley, red with tomatoes or beets, yellow with saffron, orange with carrot, brown with whole wheat or buckwheat, even black with squid's ink!

Decisions, decisions. It's no wonder most of us just break down and settle for the tried-and-true spaghetti, linguini, fettuccine, or macaroni.

Feel free to stick to tried-and-true pastas when you prepare the sauces in this book. But also feel free to experiment: there is no *one* right pasta for any of the recipes; all make excellent toppings for any number of different pasta varieties.

Of course, there are certain pastas that better suit a particular sauce than others. On the whole, lighter sauces—a fresh tomato sauce, perhaps, or a cream sauce with delicately sliced vegetables—go better with lighter, more delicate pasta strands. More robust sauces such as a classic Bolognese or a thick cheese sauce are better partnered with heartier, broader noodles. And thick, chunky sauces full of meats or vegetables may go best with larger shapes such as shells. It's simple logic.

PASTA VARIETIES

To aid you in your choice of pasta for a particular sauce, I have grouped by shape category some of the pasta varieties you're likely to encounter when shopping. Wherever the English name is more common than the Italian, I have used it.

Strands

Angel Hair. Extra-fine strands. In Italian, *capelli d'angelo.*

Bavette. Like spaghetti, only oval in cross section.

Bucatini. Thin, spaghettilike strands with holes through the center.

Fedelini. Very thin spaghetti.

Fusilli. "Fuses." Thin, squiggly, spaghettilike strands.

Perciatelli. About twice as thick as spaghetti, with a hole running through its center.

Spaghetti. The most familiar stringlike pasta.

Vermicelli. Literally, "little worms." A very thin spaghetti.

Ribbons

Fettuccine. Ribbons about ¼ inch wide.

Fettuccelli. A narrower form of fettuccine.

Fettucci. Ribbons about ½ inch wide.

Linguini. Very narrow, thick ribbons, almost like a flattened spaghetti.

Mafalde. A wide ribbon with a rippled edge.

Papardelle. Wide, short ribbons.

Tagliarini. Small, thin tagliatelli.

Tagliatelli. Similar to fettuccine, only generally somewhat wider.

Shapes

Bocconcini. Grooved tubes about 1½ inches long and ½ inch in diameter.

Bow Ties. Shaped exactly like the name implies; vary in size.

Cannolicchi. Small, ridged tubes.

Cavatelli. A narrow shell with a rippled surface.

Conchiglie. Conch-shell shapes, varying in size and sometimes grooved.

Ditali. Short macaroni tubes.

Farfalle. Literally, "butterflies." A shape related to bow ties.

Gemelli. "Twins." Two short strands twined together.

Gnocchi. Small pasta dumplings.

Lumachi. Small, snail-shaped shells.

Macaroni. In general, any tubular pasta with a hole through the center. In practice, this term is used most often for *elbow* macaroni, small to medium sized, short, curved tubes.

Maruzze. Shells, varying in size from small to very large, sometimes smooth, sometimes ridged.

Mostaccioli. "Little moustaches," these 2-inch medium tubes have diagonally cut ends. Sometimes grooved.

Penne. Short, narrow tubes with ends cut diagonally like a quill pen. Sometimes grooved.

Rigatoni. Large grooved tubes.

Ruote. Shaped like a wagon wheel.

Rotelli. Corkscrewlike spirals.

Ziti. Large macaronilike tubes cut into short lengths.

Filled Pastas

Agnolotti. Small, turnover-shaped semicircles.

Cappelletti. Little stuffed hat shapes.

Ravioli. The familiar stuffed pasta squares.

Tortellini. Small crescent shapes closed into a circle.

COOKING PASTA

Whenever possible, follow manufacturer's package instructions for cooking any particular form of pasta. These general guidelines will help you get good results:

- Use a large quantity of water relative to the amount of pasta you are cooking. There should be plenty of room for the pasta to move around as it boils so that it doesn't stick together.
- To help prevent sticking, add a splash of oil—generally olive oil is best—to the water before you add the pasta.
- Salt is optional in the cooking water.
- Fish out a strand or piece of pasta with a long fork near the end of the cooking time to test for doneness. Pasta cooked *al dente*, cooked through but still slightly chewy, is the preferred way to eat it. Cooking time will vary with the size and shape of pasta and how dry it is.
- Drain the cooked pasta thoroughly. If you like, toss it with a little olive oil or butter to keep it from sticking before you add the sauce. Serve immediately.

PASTA PORTIONS

All of the recipes in this book yield enough sauce for four to six servings. I have based the quantities on a cooked pasta portion of 1 to 1½ cups.

A GUIDE TO BASIC INGREDIENTS

There are several basic ingredients I always keep on hand for pasta sauces—which are, in fact, essentials in any well-stocked kitchen cupboard:

Butter. I use only unsalted (sweet) butter, which has a fresher, purer flavor than the salted variety and leaves *you* the option of salting any dish to taste. There are many good varieties of unsalted butter on the market. Buy it in quantity and keep the excess butter in the freezer.

Cheeses. A good Parmesan cheese for grating is absolutely indispensable for most pasta meals. Many supermarkets carry whole, ungrated Parmesan that you can buy in pieces of any size you choose; if not, seek out a good Italian deli. Do *not* use commercial, ready-grated Parmesan (though some delis do sell good cheese freshly grated). Look for Parmesan with a good golden color, avoiding paler cheeses that have not been aged sufficiently. Store it in the refrigerator, wrapped in plastic wrap; refrigerate already grated cheese in an airtight container.

Romano, the sheep's milk version of Parmesan, has a sharper flavor and makes an excellent alternative.

Garlic. Buy whole heads of garlic and store them in a dry, airy place. Powdered garlic and garlic salt are really unacceptable substitutes. To peel a garlic clove easily, separate it from the head and place it on the work surface. Place the side of a broad-bladed knife on top and hit down firmly—but not too hard—to crush the clove slightly. The skin will then slip off, leaving the garlic clove ready for chopping.

Herbs. Dried oregano is the single most essential herb for pasta sauces. Dried thyme, rosemary, and basil also come in handy frequently, as do bay leaves. Keep all herbs in airtight jars, stored away from light in a cool, dry place.

Fresh herbs add wonderful variety to sauces. Basil and parsley in particular are necessary for many classic recipes. Most good-sized supermarkets now carry a wide selection of fresh herbs.

Oil. The rich, fruity flavor of olive oil gives distinctive character to any number of pasta sauces. Choose only extra-virgin olive oil, extracted from the fruit on the first pressing without heat or chemicals; the labels of good-quality products will make this clear to you. Among extra-virgin oils, you'll still find great variety, with some almost a pale golden color, others very dark and green. Generally, the darker the oil, the more distinctive will be its fruity olive flavor; lighter oils are less assertive. I prefer dark olive oils, simply because I like that flavor to come through; if you do not, opt for a lighter oil or substitute some flavorless vegetable oil for part of the olive oil in a recipe.

Store olive oil in its airtight container, away from light and heat.

Tomato Concentrate and Paste. This is an essential flavor enhancer for many sauces. I am very partial to Italian double-strength tomato concentrate, usually sold in 4½-ounce tubes and now widely available. It is really twice as strong and flavorful as canned tomato paste; and unlike the cans, the tubes reseal with their twist-on caps and keep in the refrigerator for weeks. If you can't find the concentrate, substitute twice the amount of canned tomato paste.

Tomatoes. Except for the few summer months when tomatoes are wonderfully ripe, flavorful, and inexpensive, canned tomatoes are the best choice for pasta sauces. I keep a good supply of cans of whole peeled tomatoes, both the 14-ounce and the 28-ounce sizes. I don't use cans of seasoned tomatoes, tomato sauce, or crushed tomatoes; I like the option of doing any seasoning or crushing myself as I prepare the recipe. Most supermarkets offer many different choices in whole canned tomatoes: national brands, Italian imports, store brands, and plain wrap. They will vary in terms of cost, size of the tomatoes, and flavor, though there's never any huge difference. The best advice is to experiment and find one whose flavor you like at a cost that's right for you.

A NOTE ON COOKING TIMES

While I've tried to keep the cooking time in every recipe to less than 30 minutes, please keep in mind all cooking times are approximate. They will vary with the size and kinds of cooking utensils you use and the peculiarities of your own stove. A sauce will reduce far more quickly in a large, wide saucepan than in a small, narrow one with less surface area.

1
SEAFOOD SAUCES

GOLDEN CAVIAR WITH BUTTER AND CHIVES

CRAB BUTTER

SIMPLE CLAM

CREAMY CLAM

RED CLAM

MUSSELS IN SAFFRON CREAM

OYSTERS IN CHAMPAGNE CREAM

SCALLOPS AND MUSHROOMS IN MARTINI CREAM

GRILLED SCALLOPS WITH
ROASTED RED BELL PEPPER PUREE

GRILLED SHRIMP WITH YELLOW BELL PEPPER CREAM

HERBED SHRIMP CREAM
SHRIMP SCAMPI
SALMON AND DILL CREAM
SALMON CROQUETTES WITH LEMON-HERB CREAM
ANCHOVIES AND ROASTED PEPPERS
TUNA, GREEN OLIVE, AND TOMATO
TUNA-CAPER CREAM
TUNA AND WHITE BEANS
MIXED SEAFOOD TOMATO

GOLDEN CAVIAR WITH BUTTER AND CHIVES

Like many elegant things, this topping is simplicity itself. Though luxurious, golden caviar—domestic whitefish roe—is relatively inexpensive. If you really want to splurge, of course, you can buy a small tin of beluga, ossetra, or sevruga.
Serve with the most delicate angel hair pasta.

- 1½ cups (3 sticks) unsalted butter, cut into pieces
- ½ cup golden caviar
- 3 tablespoons chopped chives

In a saucepan, melt the butter over moderate heat. As soon as it has melted, pour it over individual portions of cooked pasta. Top each serving with a generous dollop of caviar and a scattering of chives.

Serves 4-6

CRAB BUTTER

You can make this simple sauce with fresh-cooked crabmeat from the fish counter, or canned. Serve with delicate to medium strands of pasta—angel hair, spaghettini, spaghetti, linguini.

- ½ pound crabmeat, flaked
- 10 tablespoons (1¼ sticks) unsalted butter
- 3 tablespoons lemon juice
- 2 tablespoons chopped fresh chives
- ½ teaspoon salt
- ½ teaspoon freshly ground white pepper

Put all the ingredients in a food processor fitted with the metal blade. Turning the machine on and off rapidly, pulse the ingredients a few times. Scrape down the work bowl and then process continuously until smooth.

Put the crab butter in a large skillet. As soon as the pasta is cooked and drained, add it to the skillet and toss thoroughly over moderate-to-low heat until the pasta is evenly coated.

Serves 4–6

SIMPLE CLAM

This is the basic "white" clam sauce served at Italian restaurants. It's wonderfully garlicky with lots of juice to spoon up or sop with bread. It's fine made with canned clams.

Serve with medium strands of pasta such as spaghetti or linguini.

9 tablespoons olive oil
6 medium-to-large garlic cloves, finely chopped
3 10¼-ounce cans whole baby clams, drained
6 tablespoons chopped fresh parsley
1¼ cups bottled clam juice
2 tablespoons dried oregano
2 tablespoons dried basil
1½ teaspoons crushed red pepper flakes (optional)
¾ teaspoon salt
¾ teaspoon freshly ground black pepper

In a large skillet, heat the oil over moderate heat. Add the garlic and sauté until it just begins to turn golden, 3 to 4 minutes.

Add the clams and parsley; sauté for 1 minute more. Then add the remaining ingredients and gently boil for about 3 minutes before pouring over cooked pasta.

Serves 4–6

CREAMY CLAM

A richer version of the basic clam sauce, serve this with medium strands of pasta such as spaghetti or linguini.

6½ tablespoons unsalted butter
6 medium garlic cloves, finely chopped
6 medium shallots, finely chopped
1 cup dry white wine
3 cups cream
½ pound shelled baby clams, drained
3 tablespoons chopped fresh parsley
Salt and freshly ground white pepper

In a large saucepan, melt the butter over moderate heat. Add the garlic and shallots. Sauté until tender, 2 to 3 minutes.

Add the wine and raise heat. Gently boil the wine until it reduces by half, 5 to 7 minutes. Add the cream and continue simmering until thick and reduced by about a third, 10 to 15 minutes more.

Stir in the clams and simmer 2 to 3 minutes more. Add the parsley and season with salt and white pepper to taste before pouring over cooked pasta.

Serves 4-6

RED CLAM

Some people—myself included—prefer clam sauce with a tomato base. Yet this version doesn't stint on the signature ingredient of clam sauces—garlic.
Serve over medium strands of pasta such as spaghetti or linguini.

¼ **cup olive oil**
8 **medium garlic cloves, finely chopped**
1 **medium onion, finely chopped**
1 **medium green bell pepper, stemmed, seeded, and cut into ¼-inch pieces**
1 **28-ounce can whole tomatoes**
1 **tablespoon double-concentrate tomato paste**
2 **teaspoons dried oregano**
1 **teaspoon dried basil**
1 **teaspoon sugar**
½ **teaspoon crushed red pepper flakes**
½ **teaspoon salt**
½ **pound shelled baby clams, drained**

In a large skillet or saucepan, heat the olive oil over moderate heat. Add the garlic, onion, and green pepper; sauté until just tender, 2 to 3 minutes.

Add the tomatoes, breaking them up with your hands. Stir in the tomato paste, herbs, sugar, red pepper flakes, and salt. Bring to a boil, reduce heat, and simmer until thick, 15 to 20 minutes. Stir in the clams and simmer 2 to 3 minutes more. Pour over cooked pasta and serve immediately.

Serves 4-6

MUSSELS IN SAFFRON CREAM

Mussels and saffron are a classic pairing. Buy the smallest mussels you can find. Many good supermarkets carry canned or frozen fish stock or broth, which is perfect for this recipe.

Serve over delicate strands of pasta such as angel hair or spaghettini.

3 cups cream
¼ teaspoon saffron strands
¼ cup unsalted butter
4 medium shallots, finely chopped
3 cups fish broth
6 dozen small fresh mussels in the shell (about 1¾ pounds), scrubbed and bearded
Salt and freshly ground white pepper

Put the cream in a bowl and crumble in the saffron. Stir and set aside.

In a saucepan or pot large enough to hold all the mussels, melt the butter over moderate heat. Add the shallots and sauté just until tender, 2 to 3 minutes. Add the broth and bring it to a boil, then reduce heat to maintain a slow simmer.

Add the mussels in their shells. Cover the pan and steam the mussels, turning them over once or twice with a wooden spoon, until they're all opened, 5 to 7 minutes.

Drain off the broth and strain it through a double thickness of cheesecloth. Set it aside. When the mussels are cool enough to handle, shell them, discarding any unopened ones.

Return the broth to the pan and bring it back to a boil. Gently boil until reduced by half, 7 to 10 minutes. Add the saffron cream, bring to a boil, and continue gently boiling until thick and reduced by about a third, about 10 minutes more. Add salt and white pepper to taste.

Reduce the heat and add the shelled mussels to the sauce. Simmer for 1 minute more, then pour over cooked pasta.

Serves 4–6

OYSTERS IN CHAMPAGNE CREAM

Delicately poached in champagne and finished with cream, plump oysters make a simple but elegant pasta topping. You can buy excellent oysters already shucked and packed in glass jars. If you don't have any champagne, dry white wine will do.
Serve over delicate strands of pasta such as angel hair or linguini.

- **4 tablespoons unsalted butter**
- **4 medium shallots, finely chopped**
- **2 cups dry champagne**
- **2 cups shucked medium oysters, drained (about 2 dozen)**
- **2 cups heavy cream**
- **1 teaspoon salt**
- **1½ tablespoons chopped fresh chives**

In a large skillet or saucepan, melt the butter over moderate heat. Add the shallots and sauté them until tender, 2 to 3 minutes. Add the champagne and bring it to a slow simmer.

Add the oysters and poach them for 2 minutes. Remove them with a slotted spoon and set aside.

Bring the champagne to a full boil and reduce it by half, letting it cook 7 to 10 minutes. Add the cream and salt and continue boiling until thick and reduced by about a third, about 10 minutes more.

Reduce the heat to a slow simmer, and add the oysters. Simmer for 1 minute more, then pour over pasta and garnish with chives.

Serves 4–6

SCALLOPS AND MUSHROOMS IN MARTINI CREAM

The two main ingredients in this dish—bay scallops and button mushrooms—are natural partners. This cream sauce made with a hint of gin and vermouth makes an excellent setting for them.

Serve over fine strands of pasta such as angel hair or spaghettini.

- ½ cup (1 stick) unsalted butter, cut into pieces
- 6 ounces button mushrooms, cut into ¼-inch-thick slices
- 6 medium shallots, finely chopped
- 4 medium garlic cloves, finely chopped
- 4½ cups heavy cream
- 2 tablespoons gin
- 1 tablespoon dry vermouth
- ¾ teaspoon salt
- ¾ pound bay scallops

In a large saucepan or skillet, melt the butter over moderate heat. Add the mushrooms, shallots, and garlic; sauté until tender, 2 to 3 minutes.

Add the cream, gin, vermouth, and salt. Raise the heat and gently boil until the mixture is thick and reduced by a third to a half, 15 to 20 minutes.

Stir in the scallops and simmer 2 to 3 minutes more. Serve immediately over cooked pasta.

Serves 4-6

GRILLED SCALLOPS WITH ROASTED RED BELL PEPPER PUREE

Dramatic and elegant as this dish is, it's very simple to prepare. If you like, you can substitute shrimp for the scallops or Yellow Bell Pepper Cream (see following recipe) for the sauce used here.
Serve over delicate angel hair pasta.

 5 medium red bell peppers
⅔ cup plus 3 tablespoons olive oil
⅔ cup fresh dill
 3 tablespoons plus 1½ teaspoons lemon juice
1¾ teaspoons salt
1¼ teaspoons freshly ground white pepper
18 large sea scallops (about 1¼ pounds)

Roast the peppers on a baking sheet in a 500°F oven until their skins are evenly blistered and browned, about 25 minutes. When they're cool enough to handle, peel, stem, and seed them, reserving their juices.

Preheat the broiler.

Put the peppers and their juices in a food processor fitted with the metal blade. Add ⅔ cup oil, the dill, lemon juice, 1¼ teaspoons salt, and ¾ teaspoon white pepper. Process until smooth.

Rub the scallops with the remaining oil and season with the remaining salt and white pepper. Broil them 4 to 5 inches from the flame until golden on the outside, but still juicy and slightly pink within, 1 to 2 minutes per side.

Spoon the sauce over individual servings of cooked pasta and place the scallops on top. Serve immediately.

Serves 4–6

GRILLED SHRIMP WITH YELLOW BELL PEPPER CREAM

If you like, you can substitute scallops for the shrimp or Roasted Red Bell Pepper Puree (see preceding recipe) for the sauce used here. Serve over angel hair pasta.

- 5 medium yellow bell peppers
- ⅔ cup heavy cream
- ⅔ cup fresh cilantro leaves
- 1¾ teaspoons salt
- 1¼ teaspoons freshly ground white pepper
- 18 large shrimp (about 1⅓ pounds), peeled and deveined
- 3 tablespoons unsalted butter, melted
- ¼ cup chopped fresh chives

Roast the yellow bell peppers on a baking sheet in a 500°F oven until their skins are evenly blistered and browned, about 25 minutes. When they're cool enough to handle, peel, stem, and seed them, reserving their juices.

Preheat the broiler.

Put the peppers and their juices in a food processor fitted with the metal blade. Add the cream, cilantro, 1¼ teaspoons salt, and ¾ teaspoon white pepper. Process until smooth.

Rub the shrimp with the butter and season with the remaining salt and white pepper. Broil them 4 to 5 inches from the heat until golden on the outside but still juicy within, 1 to 2 minutes per side.

Spoon the sauce over individual servings of cooked pasta and place the shrimp on top. Garnish with chives and serve immediately.

Serves 4–6

HERBED SHRIMP CREAM

Tiny bay shrimp combine in this recipe with fresh fines herbes and a white wine cream sauce. Serve over fine to medium strands of pasta such as angel hair, spaghetti, or linguini.

½ cup (1 stick) unsalted butter, cut into pieces
4 medium shallots, finely chopped
1 quart heavy cream
2 cups dry white wine
1 pound peeled bay shrimp, precooked
1 tablespoon lemon juice
1 tablespoon chopped fresh dill
1 tablespoon chopped fresh tarragon leaves
2 teaspoons chopped fresh parsley
2 teaspoons chopped fresh chives
¾ teaspoon salt

In a large skillet or saucepan, melt the butter over moderate heat. Add the shallots, and sauté until tender, 2 to 3 minutes.

Add the cream and white wine, raise the heat, and boil briskly until the sauce is thick and reduced by about half, 15 to 20 minutes.

Stir in the shrimp and remaining ingredients. Simmer until heated through, 1 to 2 minutes, before pouring over cooked pasta.

Serves 4–6

SHRIMP SCAMPI

This classic method of sautéing shrimp adapts perfectly for making a pasta sauce. Lots of garlic is essential. Serve over spaghetti or linguini.

- 1½ cups olive oil
- ½ cup (1 stick) unsalted butter, cut into pieces
- 8 medium-to-large garlic cloves, finely chopped
- 1½ tablespoons crushed red pepper flakes
- 36 medium shrimp (about ¾ pound), shelled and deveined
- 1 green bell pepper, stemmed, seeded, and cut into ¼-inch pieces
- 1 red bell pepper, stemmed, seeded, and cut into ¼-inch pieces
- ⅓ cup lemon juice
- ¼ cup chopped fresh parsley
- 1½ teaspoons salt

In a large skillet, heat the olive oil and the butter over moderate-to-high heat. Add the garlic and pepper flakes; sauté for about 30 seconds.

Add the shrimp and diced green and red peppers; sauté for 2 to 3 minutes, until the shrimp turn pink and are just cooked through. Carefully stir in the lemon juice, parsley, and salt. Serve immediately over cooked pasta.

Serves 4–6

SALMON AND DILL CREAM

Use a good quality, fairly dry, and lean smoked salmon (deli lox is too fatty for this recipe). Serve over angel hair or other delicate pasta.

- **3 tablespoons unsalted butter**
- **3 medium shallots, finely chopped**
- **¾ pound thinly sliced smoked salmon, cut into ½-by-1-inch pieces**
- **3 cups heavy cream**
- **3 tablespoons chopped fresh dill**
- **¾ teaspoon white pepper**

In a medium-to-large saucepan, melt the butter over moderate heat. Add the shallots and sauté until tender, 2 to 3 minutes. Add the salmon and sauté 2 to 3 minutes more. Empty the pan, reserving the salmon-shallot mixture.

Add the cream to the pan and bring it to a boil over moderate-to-high heat. Gently boil until it can coat the back of a wooden spoon, 15 to 20 minutes. Add the reserved salmon mixture and gently boil about 2 minutes more. Then stir in the dill and white pepper. Serve immediately over cooked pasta.

Serves 4–6

SALMON CROQUETTES WITH LEMON-HERB CREAM

This is sensational made with alderwood-smoked salmon that comes in a can. If you can't find that, use regular canned salmon, which also is excellent.

Serve over medium-to-broad strands or ribbons of pasta such as spaghetti, linguini, or fettuccine.

SALMON CROQUETTES

3 6¼-ounce cans alder-smoked salmon, skin and bones removed

1½ cups fresh white bread crumbs

3 eggs

3 medium garlic cloves

3 medium shallots, coarsely chopped

1½ teaspoons lemon juice

1½ teaspoons salt

¾ teaspoon freshly ground white pepper

3 tablespoons chopped fresh chives

6 tablespoons unsalted butter

3 tablespoons olive oil

LEMON-HERB CREAM SAUCE

3 tablespoons unsalted butter
3 medium shallots, finely chopped
3 cups heavy cream
6 tablespoons lemon juice
3 tablespoons chopped fresh chives
3 tablespoons chopped fresh dill
3 tablespoons chopped fresh parsley

To make the croquettes, put the salmon, bread crumbs, eggs, garlic, shallots, lemon juice, salt, and white pepper in a food processor fitted with the metal blade. Turning the machine on and off rapidly, pulse the ingredients several times. Scrape down the work bowl and then process until ingredients are finely chopped. Pulse in the chives.

In a large skillet, heat the butter and oil over moderate heat. Moisten your hands and shape the salmon mixture into 1-inch oblongs to make about 30 croquettes. Add them to the skillet in batches and sauté them until golden brown on all sides, about 5 minutes per batch. Set them aside to drain on paper towels.

Pour off the fat from the skillet. Melt the butter for the sauce over moderate heat. Add the shallots and sauté until tender, 2 to 3 minutes. Add the cream and lemon juice; gently boil until the sauce is thick, 10 to 15 minutes.

Stir the herbs into the sauce and then add the salmon croquettes. Simmer gently for 3 to 5 minutes more, until heated through. Serve immediately over cooked pasta.

Serves 4-6

ANCHOVIES AND ROASTED PEPPERS

A favorite antipasto becomes a quick, simple pasta topping. If you like, you can use canned or bottled roasted Italian red peppers instead of roasting them yourself.

Serve over medium strands or ribbons of pasta—spaghetti, linguini, fettuccine—or with medium shells or other shapes.

> 9 medium red bell peppers
> 1 cup olive oil
> 5 medium garlic cloves, finely chopped
> 8 2-ounce cans anchovy fillets, drained and separated
> 1¼ cups plus 2 tablespoons chopped fresh parsley
> Freshly ground black pepper
> Grated Parmesan cheese

Roast the peppers on a baking sheet in a 500°F oven until their skins are evenly blistered and browned, about 25 minutes. When they're cool enough to handle, peel, stem, and seed them, reserving their juices. Cut or tear the peppers into ½-inch-wide strips.

In a large skillet, heat the oil over moderate-to-high heat. Add the garlic and sauté 1 minute. Add the roasted peppers and the anchovies, sauté until heated through, about 2 minutes more.

Toss in the parsley, stir briefly. Serve immediately over cooked pasta with plenty of black pepper and Parmesan cheese.

Serves 4-6

TUNA, GREEN OLIVE, AND TOMATO

Green olives give this sauce a sharp, tangy flavor. For extra richness, use Italian tuna packed in olive oil.

Serve with spaghetti, fettuccine, medium shells, or other shapes.

    3 tablespoons olive oil
    3 large garlic cloves, finely chopped
    1 28-ounce can whole tomatoes
    1 tablespoon double-concentrate tomato paste
1½ teaspoons dried oregano
1½ teaspoons dried basil
    ¾ teaspoon sugar
    ¾ teaspoon salt
    3 3¼-ounce cans tuna in oil, drained and coarsely
      flaked
    ¾ cup coarsely chopped pitted green olives

In a large skillet or saucepan, heat the olive oil over moderate heat. Add the garlic and sauté until tender, 2 to 3 minutes.

Add the tomatoes, breaking them up with your hands. Stir in the tomato paste, oregano, basil, sugar, and salt. Raise the heat slightly and gently boil until fairly thick, about 15 minutes.

Stir in the tuna and olives; simmer until heated through, 1 to 2 minutes more. Serve immediately over cooked pasta.

Serves 4–6

TUNA-CAPER CREAM

This uncooked sauce was inspired by the dressing used in a classic Italian appetizer, vitello tonnato—*cold roasted or poached veal topped with a rich, smooth cream sauce made of tuna, garlic, mayonnaise, and capers.*

Serve over medium strands or ribbons of pasta such as spaghetti, linguini, tagliatelli, or fettuccine.

    2 6½ ounce and 1 3¼-ounce cans tuna in oil, drained
       and coarsely flaked
    4 medium garlic cloves, peeled and coarsely
       chopped
    ¾ cup plus 2 tablespoons mayonnaise
    ½ cup plus 1 tablespoon olive oil
    6 tablespoons chopped fresh parsley
    ¼ cup drained capers
    2½ tablespoons lemon juice
    1 teaspoon salt
    1 teaspoon freshly ground black pepper

Put the tuna and garlic in a food processor fitted with the metal blade. Turning the machine on and off rapidly, pulse the ingredients a few times until coarsely chopped. Scrape down the work bowl.

Add the mayonnaise, olive oil, 4 tablespoons parsley, and the remaining ingredients. Process until smooth.

Spoon the sauce over cooked pasta the instant the pasta is drained. Toss well and garnish with the remaining parsley.

Serves 4–6

TUNA AND WHITE BEANS

Tonno e fagioli *is a popular antipasto. It also makes a great, quick topping for pasta.*

Serve over spaghetti, linguini, tagliatelli, fettuccine, or with medium shells, bow ties, or other shapes.

2 14½-ounce cans cannellini (white kidney beans), rinsed and drained
1 cup olive oil
½ cup lemon juice
4 medium garlic cloves, finely chopped
¼ cup chopped fresh parsley
1 teaspoon salt
1 6½-ounce can tuna in oil, drained, at room temperature
2 medium scallions, coarsely chopped
Freshly ground black pepper

In a large skillet or saucepan, combine the beans, olive oil, lemon juice, garlic, parsley, and salt. Cook over low-to-moderate heat until the beans are hot, about 5 minutes.

Spoon the beans over cooked pasta. Break the tuna on top in coarse chunks. Garnish with scallions and plenty of black pepper.

Serves 4–6

MIXED SEAFOOD TOMATO

Use whatever combination of fresh fish and shellfish you like. Serve with pasta shells or over medium strands of pasta such as spaghetti or linguini.

       3 tablespoons olive oil
       3 medium shallots, finely chopped
       3 medium garlic cloves, finely chopped
       1 large green bell pepper, stemmed, seeded, and cut
          into ½-inch pieces
    1½ cups fish broth
       1 28-ounce can whole tomatoes
       2 tablespoons double-concentrate tomato paste
       2 teaspoons sugar
    1½ teaspoons dried oregano
    1½ teaspoons fennel seed
       ¾ teaspoon salt
       2 bay leaves
       ⅓ pound halibut fillet, cut into ½-inch pieces
       ⅓ pound bay scallops
       ⅓ pound bay shrimp, peeled and deveined

In a large skillet or saucepan, heat the oil over moderate heat. Add the shallots, garlic, and green pepper; sauté about 2 minutes. Add the fish broth, raise the heat slightly, and gently boil until reduced by about a third, 5 to 7 mintues.

Add the tomatoes, breaking them up with your hands. Stir in the tomato paste, sugar, oregano, fennel, salt, and bay leaves. Gently boil until the sauce is fairly thick but some liquid remains, 12 to 15 minutes more.

Add the seafood and simmer until it is just cooked through, about 5 minutes more, stirring gently. Remove the bay leaves and serve immediately over cooked pasta.

Serves 4-6

2
POULTRY AND MEAT SAUCES

SMOKED CHICKEN WITH GOAT CHEESE AND PINE NUTS

CHICKEN WITH SPICY SESAME-PEANUT CREAM

CHICKEN PAPRIKASH

CHICKEN LIVER SAUTE

CHICKEN WITH LEMON-CAPER CREAM

TURKEY WITH PEPPERS, OLIVES, AND TOMATO

BOLOGNESE

QUICK CHILI

BEEF TENDERLOIN WITH SPRING VEGETABLES AND CREAM

BEEF AND ONION RAGOUT

VEAL AND TARRAGON TOMATO CREAM

VEAL AND MUSHROOM RAGOUT

VEAL SAUSAGE IN MUSTARD CREAM

BACON AND GARLIC SAUTE

PROSCIUTTO WITH BUTTER, SAGE, AND PARMESAN CHEESE

HOT BACON VINAIGRETTE

BACON AND GREEN OLIVES

PUTANESCA

CARBONARA

HAM, TOMATO, AND SAGE

SPICY SAUSAGE

SAUSAGE AND MOZZARELLA IN TOMATO CREAM

PORK AND CARROT RAGOUT

CHINESE MINCED PORK

SAUSAGE AND NEW POTATOES

CHUNKY MEAT AND ZUCCHINI

PARMESAN-HERB MEATBALLS WITH TOMATO

LAMB MEATBALLS WITH RED LENTILS

SMOKED CHICKEN WITH GOAT CHEESE AND PINE NUTS

This is a satisfying combination of textures and tastes. Many delis carry smoked chicken breast (smoked turkey breast, even more widely available, is a good substitute). If you can, buy it whole and cut it up yourself.
Serve over medium ribbons of pasta such as fettuccine.

- ¾ **cup shelled pine nuts**
- 3 **tablespoons unsalted butter**
- 2 **medium shallots, finely chopped**
- 1 **cup heavy cream**
- ½ **pound fresh goat cheese, cut into chunks**
- **Pinch nutmeg**
- 1 **pound smoked chicken breast, skinned and cut crosswise into ¼-inch-wide strips**
- 3 **tablespoons chopped fresh chives**

Spread the pine nuts on a baking sheet and toast them in a 450°F oven until golden brown, about 10 minutes; watch them carefully to guard against burning.

Meanwhile, in a medium saucepan, melt the butter over moderate heat. Add the shallots and sauté until tender, 2 to 3 minutes. Add the cream and bring it to a boil. Add the goat cheese and nutmeg. Reduce the heat and simmer, stirring continuously, until the cheese just melts.

Stir in the chicken pieces and simmer about 5 minutes more. Serve immediately over cooked pasta. Sprinkle with pine nuts and chives.

Serves 4–6

CHICKEN WITH SPICY SESAME-PEANUT CREAM

This is an easy-to-make version of a typical Szechuan-style topping. The Asian food sections of most good-sized markets carry the sesame paste and hot chili oil required.

Serve over Chinese egg noodles. Or, if you prefer, use ribbons of pasta such as spaghetti, tagliatelli, or fettuccine.

- ¼ cup peanut or vegetable oil
- 1 pound boned and skinned chicken breasts, cut crosswise into ½-inch-wide strips
- ¼ cup blanched peanuts
- 2 medium garlic cloves, finely chopped
- 2 tablespoons finely chopped fresh ginger
- ½ cup sesame paste
- 6 tablespoons peanut butter
- 6 tablespoons soy sauce
- 2 tablespoons hot chili oil
- 2 tablespoons honey
- ½–1 cup cold water
- 2 medium scallions, finely chopped
- 3 tablespoons chopped fresh cilantro leaves

In a large wok or skillet, heat the oil over high heat. Add the chicken, peanuts, garlic, and ginger. Stir-fry just until the chicken is no longer pink, 3 to 4 minutes.

Reduce the heat to low and add the sesame paste, peanut butter, soy sauce, chili oil, and honey. Stir until the ingredients have melted and blended, then simmer about 3 minutes more, until the chicken is cooked through.

Stir in enough of the water to thin the sauce to a smooth coating consistency. Gently boil, then serve immediately over cooked pasta. Garnish with scallions and cilantro.

Serves 4–6

CHICKEN PAPRIKASH

This luxurious Hungarian-style dish is traditionally served alongside spaetzle—little boiled noodle-dough dumplings—or broad egg noodles. For a one-dish meal, it's perfect served on pasta.

Serve with medium-to-wide ribbons of pasta, over shells, or over other medium-to-large pasta shapes.

- **6 tablespoons unsalted butter**
- **2 tablespoons vegetable oil**
- **1 pound boned and skinned chicken breasts, cut crosswise into ½-inch-wide strips**
- **1 medium green or red bell pepper, quartered, stemmed, seeded, and cut crosswise into ¼-inch-wide strips**
- **1 medium onion, finely chopped**
- **2 tablespoons paprika**
- **1 teaspoon caraway seed**
- **½ cup dry white wine**
- **2 tablespoons lemon juice**
- **1 cup sour cream**
- **2 teaspoons double-concentrate tomato paste**
- **1 teaspoon salt**
- **½ teaspoon freshly ground black pepper**

In a large skillet or saucepan, melt the butter with the oil over moderate-to-high heat. When the butter foams, add the chicken, green or red pepper, and onion. Sauté until the chicken has lost all its pink color and the vegetables are tender-crisp, about 5 minutes.

Add the paprika and caraway seed; sauté 1 minute more. Add the wine and lemon juice; gently boil, stirring and scraping the pan, for about 5 minutes.

Stir in the sour cream, tomato paste, salt, and black pepper. Reduce the heat to low and simmer for 2 to 3 minutes more. Serve immediately over cooked pasta.

Serves 4–6

CHICKEN LIVER SAUTE

A rapid sauté of chicken livers makes a fine, country-style topping. Serve over medium strands of pasta, such as fettuccine, or over medium pasta shells.

- **1 tablespoon unsalted butter**
- **2 medium garlic cloves, finely chopped**
- **1 medium onion, coarsely chopped**
- **4 strips (about ¼ pound) smoked bacon, cut crosswise into ⅛-inch-wide strips**
- **1 pound chicken livers, trimmed and cut into ½-inch pieces**
- **1½ cups chicken broth**
- **1 tablespoon Worcestershire sauce**
- **1 teaspoon dried thyme**
- **1 cup heavy cream**
- **¾ teaspoon salt**
- **¾ teaspoon freshly ground black pepper**
- **3 tablespoons chopped fresh parsley**

In a large skillet, melt the butter over moderate heat. Add the garlic, onion, and bacon; sauté 2 to 3 minutes. Add the chicken livers, raise the heat slightly, and sauté until they are lightly browned, about 3 minutes more. Remove the chicken livers from the skillet, set them aside, and drain off the fat from the pan.

Add the chicken broth, Worcestershire sauce, and thyme. Bring this to a boil and continue until reduced by about half, about 10 minutes. Add the cream, salt, and black pepper; simmer until the sauce has thickened, 7 to 10 minutes more.

Return the chicken livers to the skillet and simmer for about 3 minutes more. Serve immediately over cooked pasta. Garnish with parsley.

Serves 4-6

CHICKEN WITH LEMON-CAPER CREAM

To make the preparation quicker, buy the prepackaged, boned, and skinned chicken breasts available in supermarket meat sections. Serve over medium ribbons of pasta such as fettuccine or tagliatelli.

¼ **cup unsalted butter**
4 **medium shallots, finely chopped**
1 **pound boned and skinned chicken breasts, cut crosswise into ½-inch-wide strips**
½ **cup lemon juice**
2 **cups heavy cream**
¼ **cup drained capers**
¼ **cup chopped fresh parsley**

In a large skillet, melt the butter over moderate heat. Add the shallots and sauté for 1 minute. Raise the heat, add the chicken pieces, and sauté until they are lightly browned, 3 to 5 minutes.

Add the lemon juice; stir and scrape the bottom of the pan with a wooden spoon to remove any lumps or browned bits. When most of the lemon juice has evaporated, add the cream. Gently boil until thick, 10 to 12 minutes.

Stir in the capers and serve immediately over cooked pasta. Garnish with chopped parsley.

Serves 4-6

TURKEY WITH PEPPERS, OLIVES, AND TOMATO

Ground turkey is a terrific substitute for ground beef in any meat sauce. Serve with spaghetti or fettuccine, penne, or pasta shells.

    2 tablespoons olive oil
    1 medium green bell pepper, stemmed, seeded, and
      coarsely chopped
    1 medium red bell pepper, stemmed, seeded, and
      coarsely chopped
    1 medium onion, finely chopped
    1 medium garlic clove, finely chopped
    1 pound ground turkey
    1 28-ounce can whole tomatoes
    ¾ cup sliced pitted black olives
    1 tablespoon double-concentrate tomato paste
    2 teaspoons sugar
    ½ teaspoon salt
    ½ teaspoon dried basil
    ½ teaspoon dried oregano
    ¼ teaspoon dried rosemary
    ¼ teaspoon crushed red pepper flakes

In a large skillet or saucepan, heat the oil over moderate heat. Add the green and red peppers, onion, and garlic. Sauté until tender, 2 to 3 minutes.

Add the turkey and raise the heat slightly. Sauté the turkey until it has lost all its pink color and left a brown glaze on the pan, about 10 minutes.

Add the tomatoes, breaking them up with your hands. Stir and scrape the bottom of the pan with a wooden spoon to dissolve the pan deposits. Stir in the remaining ingredients and gently boil until thick, 15 to 20 minutes. Serve over cooked pasta.

Serves 4–6

BOLOGNESE

Though it is traditionally served with spaghetti, this classic Italian meat sauce goes well with virtually any type pasta.

- **6 tablespoons olive oil**
- **6 medium garlic cloves, finely chopped**
- **1 large onion, finely chopped**
- **1 pound ground beef**
- **1 28-ounce can whole tomatoes**
- **1½ tablespoons double-concentrate tomato paste**
- **1 tablespoon dried oregano**
- **1 tablespoon dried basil**
- **1½ teaspoons sugar**
- **¾ teaspoon salt**

In a large skillet or saucepan, heat the oil over moderate heat. Add the garlic and onion; sauté until tender, 2 to 3 minutes.

Add the beef and raise the heat slightly. Sauté the beef until it has lost all its pink color and left a brown glaze on the pan, about 10 minutes.

Add the tomatoes, breaking them up with your hands. Stir and scrape the bottom of the pan with a wooden spoon to dissolve the pan deposits. Stir in the remaining ingredients and gently boil until thick, 15 to 20 minutes. Serve over cooked pasta.

Serves 4-6

QUICK CHILI

Chili con carne served over pasta is a popular diner dish. This quick recipe has the rich flavor and spice of a chili that has been simmered for hours.
Serve over spaghetti, macaroni, or pasta shells.

2½ tablespoons olive oil
⅓ pound well-fatted bacon, cut crosswise into
  ¼-inch-wide strips
½ pound ground beef
3 medium garlic cloves, crushed
2 medium onions, finely chopped
2 teaspoons cumin
1½ teaspoons chili powder
1½ teaspoons cayenne
1 28-ounce can whole tomatoes
2 8¾-ounce cans kidney beans, drained
2 teaspoons sugar
2 teaspoons dried oregano
¾ teaspoon salt
8 drops hot chili sauce

In a large skillet or saucepan, heat the oil over moderate heat. Add the bacon and sauté until very lightly browned, about 2 minutes.

Add the beef, garlic, and onions. Sauté until the beef has lost all its pink color and left a brown glaze on the pan, about 10 minutes. Add the cumin, chili powder, and cayenne. Sauté about 1 minute more.

Add the tomatoes, breaking them up with your hands. Stir and scrape the bottom of the pan with a slotted spoon to dissolve the pan deposits into the sauce. Stir in the remaining ingredients and gently boil until thick, 15 to 20 minutes. Serve over cooked pasta.

Serves 4–6

BEEF TENDERLOIN WITH SPRING VEGETABLES AND CREAM

A small cut of prime tenderloin goes a long way in this elegant presentation. Use whatever seasonal vegetables you like.
Serve with medium strands of pasta—spaghetti, spaghettini, or linguini.

　　3 **cups beef broth**
　　2 **medium garlic cloves, finely chopped**
　　3 **cups heavy cream**
　1¼ **pounds beef tenderloin steak, about 1½ inches thick**
　　3 **tablespoons unsalted butter, melted**
Salt and freshly ground black pepper
　　3 **dozen small snowpeas, trimmed**
　　2 **medium zucchini, cut diagonally into ⅛-inch-thick slices**
　　1 **medium carrot, cut diagonally into ⅛-inch-thick slices**
　　1 **medium red bell pepper, stemmed, seeded, and cut crosswise into ¼-inch-wide strips**
　　3 **tablespoons chopped fresh chives**

Preheat the broiler.

In a large saucepan, combine broth and garlic. Bring to a boil. Continue boiling until liquid is reduced by half, 10 to 15 minutes. Add the cream and continue boiling until it reaches a smooth coating consistency, 10 to 15 minutes more.

Meanwhile, brush the steak with the butter and season lightly with salt and black pepper to taste. Broil the steak 4 to 5 inches from heat about 5 minutes per side for medium-rare.

After you've turned the steak, and shortly before the sauce is ready, add the vegetables to the sauce. Simmer them for about 3 minutes, until tender-crisp.

Pour the sauce over individual servings of cooked pasta, arranging the vegetables in an attractive pattern. Cut the steak on a diagonal into ¼-inch-thick slices. Place some of the slices, overlapping slightly, across the top of each serving. Garnish with chives.

Serves 4–6

BEEF AND ONION RAGOUT

This Bolognese-style sauce has the intensely rich flavor of beef and onion. Serve over spaghetti, medium-to-wide ribbons of pasta, penne, other tubes, or shells.

  ¼ cup olive oil
  1 pound ground beef
  4 medium garlic cloves, finely chopped
  3 medium onions, finely chopped
  2 cups beef broth
  1 28-ounce can whole tomatoes
  2 tablespoons double-concentrate tomato paste
  1 tablespoon sugar
  1½ teaspoons dried oregano
  1½ teaspoons dried basil
  1 teaspoon dried rosemary
  1 teaspoon dried thyme
  ¾ teaspoon salt

In a large skillet or saucepan, heat the oil over moderate-to-high heat. Add the beef, garlic, and onions. Sauté until the beef has lost all its pink color and has left a brown glaze on the pan, about 10 minutes.

Add the broth. Stir and scrape the bottom of the pan with a slotted spoon to dissolve the pan deposits into the sauce. Gently boil until most of the broth has evaporated.

Add the tomatoes, breaking them up with your hands. Stir in the remaining ingredients. Gently boil until thick, 15 to 20 minutes. Serve over cooked pasta.

Serves 4–6

VEAL AND TARRAGON TOMATO CREAM

Think of this, if you like, as an elegant, creamy version of a Bolognese sauce. Serve over fine strands of pasta—angel hair or spaghettini.

        3 tablespoons unsalted butter
        4 large shallots, finely chopped
        1 pound ground veal
        2 cups heavy cream
        2 tablespoons double-concentrate tomato paste
        1 tablespoon chopped fresh tarragon leaves
        1 tablespoon lemon juice
        1 teaspoon sugar
        ½ teaspoon salt
        ½ teaspoon freshly ground white pepper

In a large skillet, melt the butter over moderate heat. Add the shallots and sauté until tender, 2 to 3 minutes. Add the veal and sauté, breaking it up into small pieces with a wooden spoon, until it is no longer pink, about 5 minutes.

Add the remaining ingredients. Simmer until thick, about 10 minutes. Serve immediately over cooked pasta.

Serves 4–6

VEAL AND MUSHROOM RAGOUT

The thinnest veal cutlets or scaloppine, quickly sautéed with mushrooms and finished with sour cream, make an elegant pasta topping. Serve over delicate strands such as angel hair.

¼ cup unsalted butter
2 tablespoons peanut oil
2 medium shallots, finely chopped
¾ pound thin veal scallops, cut into ½-inch-wide strips
¼ pound button mushrooms, cut into ¼-inch-thick slices
¾ cup dry white wine
2 cups sour cream
¾ teaspoon salt
½ teaspoon freshly ground white pepper
2 tablespoons chopped fresh parsley
2 tablespoons chopped fresh chives

In a large skillet, melt the butter with the oil over moderate heat. Add the shallots and sauté until tender, 2 to 3 minutes.

Raise the heat and add the veal. Sauté until lightly browned, 3 to 5 minutes. Remove the veal from the skillet and add the mushrooms. Sauté until golden, then remove from the skillet.

Add the wine to the skillet. Stir and scrape the bottom of the pan with a slotted spoon to dissolve the pan deposits into the sauce. Boil until reduced by about two thirds, 7 to 10 minutes.

Add the sour cream to the skillet and return the veal and mushrooms. Reduce the heat slightly and simmer until the sauce is thick and the ingredients have heated through, 3 to 5 minutes more. Season with salt and white pepper. Spoon over cooked pasta and garnish with parsley and chives.

Serves 4–6

VEAL SAUSAGE IN MUSTARD CREAM

Veal bratwurst, browned, sliced, and served on top of pasta in a cream sauce flavored with Dijon mustard, makes a surprisingly elegant main course. Serve over thin-to-medium strands of pasta such as angel hair or spaghetti.

- 4 veal bratwursts (about 1 pound)
- 2 tablespoons unsalted butter
- 1 tablespoon vegetable oil
- 3 cups heavy cream
- 2 tablespoons Dijon-style mustard
- 1 tablespoon chopped fresh sage leaves
- ¾ teaspoon salt
- 3 tablespoons chopped fresh parsley

Put the bratwursts in a large saucepan with enough cold water to cover them. Bring the water to a boil over medium heat. As soon as the water begins to boil, drain the bratwursts and pat them dry with paper towels.

In a large skillet, melt the butter with the oil over moderate heat. Add the bratwursts and sauté them until nicely browned on all sides. Remove them from the skillet and set aside.

Add the cream to the skillet. Stir and scrape the bottom of the pan with a slotted spoon to dissolve the pan deposits into the sauce. Gently boil until the cream is reduced by half, 10 to 15 minutes.

Stir in the mustard, sage, and salt. Reduce the heat. Cut the sausages on a diagonal into ½-inch-thick slices and return them to the sauce to heat through for 1 to 2 minutes. Serve over cooked pasta and garnish with parsley.

Serves 4–6

BACON AND GARLIC SAUTE

A simple sauce for bacon lovers. Serve with spaghetti, macaroni, or pasta shells.

1 **cup plus 2 tablespoons (2¼ sticks) unsalted butter, cut into pieces**
¾ **pound sliced bacon, cut crosswise into ¼-inch-wide strips**
3 **medium garlic cloves, finely chopped**
2 **tablespoons chopped fresh parsley**
Grated Parmesan cheese

In a large skillet, melt 1 tablespoon of the butter over moderate heat. Add the bacon and sauté until crisp and golden, 3 to 5 minutes. Pour off the fat, leaving the bacon in the skillet.

Add the remaining butter, garlic, and parsley. When the butter has melted, sauté garlic and parsley for about 1 minute more. Then pour the sauce over cooked pasta. Sprinkle generously with Parmesan cheese.

Serves 4-6

PROSCIUTTO WITH BUTTER, SAGE, AND PARMESAN CHEESE

For the prosciutto, you can substitute any other dry-cured ham sliced paper-thin. Serve with spaghetti or linguini.

1¼ cups (2½ sticks) unsalted butter, cut into pieces
3 tablespoons olive oil
2 medium garlic cloves, finely chopped
¾ pound thinly sliced prosciutto, cut into ¼-by-1-inch strips
2 teaspoons coarsely chopped fresh sage leaves
Freshly ground black pepper
Grated Parmesan cheese

In a large skillet, melt the butter with the oil over moderate-to-high heat. Add the garlic and sauté for about 1 minute. Add the prosciutto and sauté until it just begins to frizzle, 2 to 3 minutes more.

Add the sage and stir well. Spoon the sauce over cooked pasta. Season with black pepper to taste and sprinkle generously with Parmesan cheese.

Serves 4–6

HOT BACON VINAIGRETTE

A little red wine vinegar added to this light, simple pasta sauce gives it the sharp edge of a good vinaigrette dressing. Balsamic vinegar makes a spectacular addition.

Serve over medium strands or ribbons of pasta such as spaghetti, linguini, or fettuccine.

1½ cups olive oil
3 medium garlic cloves, unpeeled and crushed
¾ pound sliced bacon, cut crosswise into ¼-inch-wide strips
½ cup red wine vinegar
3 tablespoons chopped fresh chives
3 tablespoons chopped fresh parsley
Freshly ground black pepper
Grated Parmesan cheese

In a large skillet, heat 3 tablespoons of the oil with the garlic over moderate heat. When the garlic sizzles and begins to brown, remove and discard it. Add the bacon and sauté until crisp and golden, 3 to 5 minutes. Pour off all the fat.

Add the vinegar to the skillet. Stir and scrape the bottom of the pan with a wooden spoon to dissolve the pan deposits. Pour in the remaining oil. As soon as the mixture is hot, stir in the chives and parsley.

Pour immediately over cooked pasta and top with plenty of black pepper and Parmesan.

Serves 4–6

BACON AND GREEN OLIVES

The smoky flavor of the bacon goes well with the sharp taste of the olives. Serve over spaghetti or pasta shells.

>   1 **cup olive oil**
>   1 **pound sliced bacon, cut crosswise into ½-inch-wide strips**
>   3 **medium garlic cloves, finely chopped**
>   1 **cup coarsely chopped pitted green olives**
>   ¼ **cup chopped fresh parsley**
>   1½ **tablespoons dried oregano**

In a large skillet, heat 2 tablespoons of the oil over moderate heat. Add the bacon and garlic; sauté until the bacon is crisp and golden, 3 to 5 minutes. Pour off all the fat.

Add the remaining oil, olives, parsley, and oregano. Sauté until heated through, 1 to 2 minutes more. Serve immediately over cooked pasta.

Serves 4-6

PUTANESCA

The name means "whore-style," an apt name for this rough, spicy, but pleasing sauce. Remove the seeds from the chilies if you want a somewhat tamer result. Serve over spaghetti, linguini, fettuccine, or pasta shells.

¼ cup olive oil
½ pound sliced bacon, cut crosswise into ½-inch-wide strips
6 medium garlic cloves, coarsely chopped
4 medium onions, coarsely chopped
3 small hot green chilies, coarsely chopped
1 28-ounce can whole tomatoes
1 tablespoon dried oregano
1 tablespoon dried basil
1 tablespoon sugar
1 teaspoon salt
1 teaspoon pepper

In a large skillet, heat the olive oil over moderate heat. Add the bacon, garlic, onions, and chilies; sauté only until the bacon begins to brown, 5 to 7 minutes.

Add the tomatoes, breaking them up with your hands. Stir in remaining ingredients. Gently boil until thick, 15 to 20 minutes. Serve over cooked pasta.

Serves 4–6

CARBONARA

This "charcoal-maker" pasta sauce is cooked by tossing it with just-cooked pasta. Serve, in the traditional style, with spaghetti.

6 tablespoons unsalted butter
¾ pound sliced bacon, cut crosswise into ¼ to ½-inch-wide strips
3 medium garlic cloves, finely chopped
6 egg yolks
2 cups heavy cream
2 cups grated Parmesan cheese
Freshly ground black pepper
¼ cup chopped fresh parsley

In a large skillet, melt the butter over moderate heat. Add the bacon and sauté until crisp, 3 to 5 minutes. Drain off all but a thin film of fat. Add the garlic and sauté about 1 minute more.

In a bowl, beat the egg yolks, cream, and 1½ cups of the Parmesan.

Add cooked, drained pasta to the skillet and pour in the cream mixture. Toss over low heat until the sauce thickens and coats the pasta, 2 to 3 minutes. Serve immediately, sprinkled generously with remaining Parmesan cheese, black pepper, and parsley.

Serves 4-6

HAM, TOMATO, AND SAGE

Although I call for Black Forest ham, you may substitute any meaty, sweet-flavored smoked ham. Serve with shells or other medium-to-large pasta shapes.

- ¼ **cup olive oil**
- 3 **medium garlic cloves, finely chopped**
- 1 **medium onion, finely chopped**
- 1¼ **pounds Black Forest ham, trimmed and cut into ½-inch cubes**
- 1 **28-ounce can whole tomatoes**
- 2½ **tablespoons finely chopped fresh sage leaves**
- 2 **teaspoons sugar**
- 1 **teaspoon freshly ground black pepper**
- ¾ **teaspoon salt**

In a large skillet or saucepan, heat the oil over moderate heat. Add the garlic and onion; sauté until tender, 2 to 3 minutes.

Add the ham and sauté about 1 minute. Then add the tomatoes, breaking them up with your hands. Stir in remaining ingredients. Gently boil until thick, 15 to 20 minutes. Serve over cooked pasta.

Serves 4–6

SPICY SAUSAGE

Available in Italian delis and some large supermarket meat counters, spicy Italian sausage becomes spicier with the addition of crushed red pepper flakes. Serve over spaghetti, linguini, or pasta shells.

                3 tablespoons olive oil
                4 large garlic cloves, finely chopped
                3 medium onions, finely chopped
                2 medium green bell peppers, stemmed, seeded, and
                    cut into ¼-inch pieces
                1 pound spicy Italian sausage, casing split and
                    removed
                1 cup dry red wine
                1 28-ounce can whole tomatoes
                2 tablespoons double-concentrate tomato paste
             1½ tablespoons dried oregano
                1 tablespoon dried basil
             1½ teaspoons crushed red pepper flakes
               ½ teaspoon salt

In a large skillet, heat the oil over moderate heat. Add the garlic, onions, and green peppers; sauté until tender, 3 to 5 minutes.

Crumble in the sausage, raise the heat slightly, and sauté until the sausage begins to brown, about 10 minutes.

Carefully pour off most of the fat. Add the wine. Stir and scrape the bottom of the pan with a wooden spoon to dissolve the pan deposits.

Add the tomatoes, breaking them up with your hands. Stir in remaining ingredients. Gently boil until thick, 15 to 20 minutes. Serve over cooked pasta.

Serves 4–6

SAUSAGE AND MOZZARELLA IN TOMATO CREAM

Eating this sauce over pasta is akin to eating a pizza-in-a-bowl. Serve over spaghetti, linguini, or pasta shells.

- ¼ cup unsalted butter
- 2 tablespoons olive oil
- ¾ pound spicy Italian sausage, casing split and removed
- 4 medium garlic cloves, finely chopped
- 2 medium onions, coarsely chopped
- 1 28-ounce can whole tomatoes
- 1 cup heavy cream
- 2½ tablespoons dried oregano
- 2 tablespoons sugar
- 1½ tablespoons double-concentrate tomato paste
- ½ teaspoon salt
- 2 bay leaves
- 1 pound mozzarella cheese, cut into ½-inch cubes

In a large skillet, melt the butter with the oil over moderate heat. Crumble in the sausage, add the garlic and onions. Sauté until the sausage just begins to brown, 7 to 10 minutes. Carefully pour off the fat.

Add the tomatoes, breaking them up with your hands. Stir in the cream, oregano, sugar, tomato paste, salt, and bay leaves. Gently boil until fairly thick, 15 to 20 minutes.

Remove the bay leaves and stir in the mozzarella cubes. Simmer just until the cheese begins to melt, about 2 minutes more. Spoon over cooked pasta.

Serves 4–6

PORK AND CARROT RAGOUT

Pork and carrot are naturally sweet. They complement each other beautifully in this appetizing, brightly colored sauce.

Serve over spaghetti, fettuccine, or other medium strands or medium ribbons of pasta.

> 5 tablespoons unsalted butter
> 4 medium onions, finely chopped
> 1 tablespoon whole fennel seed
> 1 pound ground pork
> 2 medium carrots, shredded
> 2½ cups beef broth
> 3 tablespoons double-concentrate tomato paste
> 1 teaspoon salt

In a large skillet, melt the butter over moderate heat. Add the onion and fennel seed; sauté until tender, 3 to 5 minutes. Add the pork and sauté, breaking it up with a wooden spoon, until it just begins to brown, 7 to 10 minutes. Add the carrots and sauté 2 to 3 minutes more.

Add the broth and bring it to a boil, stirring and scraping the bottom of the skillet with a slotted spoon to dissolve pan deposits into the sauce. Stir in the tomato paste and the salt; simmer until thick, about 10 minutes more. Serve over cooked pasta.

Serves 4–6

CHINESE MINCED PORK

This rich, aromatic sauce is surprisingly good over spaghetti, but it's most at home on top of Chinese egg or rice noodles.

¼ cup peanut oil
5 medium garlic cloves, finely chopped
3 tablespoons finely chopped fresh ginger
1¼ pounds ground pork
24 dried shitake mushrooms, soaked in hot water until soft, then stemmed, drained, and coarsely chopped
6 tablespoons sesame seed
1 cup black bean sauce
5 tablespoons hot chili oil
5 tablespoons rice vinegar
2½ tablespoons soy sauce (can substitute low-salt or light soy)
¾ cup chopped scallion

In a large wok or skillet, heat the oil over moderate heat. Add the garlic and ginger; stir-fry for about 1 minute. Then add the pork, mushrooms, and sesame seed. Stir-fry, breaking up the pork, until the pork just begins to brown, 5 to 7 minutes.

Add the black bean sauce, chili oil, rice vinegar, and soy sauce; simmer 2 to 3 minutes more. Serve over cooked pasta, topped with the chopped scallion.

Serves 4–6

SAUSAGE AND NEW POTATOES

A decidedly rustic sauce, this is perfect to make when the markets are full of beautiful new potatoes. Serve over shells, other medium pasta shapes, or with large macaroni.

  6 tablespoons olive oil
  ¾ pound spicy Italian sausage, casing split and removed
 16 new potatoes, washed and cut into ¼-inch-thick slices
  2 medium onions, coarsely chopped
  2 medium garlic cloves, finely chopped
  1 28-ounce can whole tomatoes
 1½ tablespoons dried oregano
  1 tablespoon double-concentrate tomato paste
  1 teaspoon sugar
  ¾ teaspoon salt
Freshly ground black pepper

In a large skillet, heat the oil over moderate heat. Crumble in the sausage; add the potatoes, onions, and garlic. Sauté until the sausage and potatoes begin to brown, 7 to 10 minutes. Carefully pour off the fat.

Add the tomatoes, breaking them up with your hands. Stir in remaining ingredients. Gently boil until thick, about 15 minutes. Serve over cooked pasta.

Serves 4-6

CHUNKY MEAT AND ZUCCHINI

You can substitute broccoli florets or carrot chunks for the zucchini, if you like, or use a mixture of vegetables. Serve with medium-to-large pasta shells.

¼ cup olive oil
2 medium garlic cloves, finely chopped
1 medium onion, coarsely chopped
1 medium green bell pepper, stemmed, seeded, and cut into ½-inch pieces
½ pound sweet Italian sausage, casing split and removed
6 ounces ground beef
1 28-ounce can whole tomatoes
4 medium zucchini, cut into ½-inch cubes
1 cup Italian cured olives, pitted and halved
2 teaspoons crushed red pepper flakes
2 teaspoons dried oregano
2 teaspoons sugar
1½ teaspoons double-concentrate tomato paste
1 teaspoon salt

In a large skillet, heat the oil over moderate heat. Add the garlic, onion, and green pepper; sauté until tender, 2 to 3 minutes.

Add the sausage and beef, breaking the meat up into coarse pieces. Sauté until browned, 7 to 10 minutes. Add the tomatoes, breaking them up with your hands. Stir in remaining ingredients. Gently boil until thick, 15 to 20 minutes. Serve over cooked pasta.

Serves 4–6

PARMESAN-HERB MEATBALLS WITH TOMATO

These remind me of the moist and aromatic meatballs you get in an old-fashioned Italian restaurant. If you like, you can use all beef or all pork in place of the mixture specified here.

Serve with spaghetti, linguini, tagliatelli, or fettuccine.

PARMESAN-HERB MEATBALLS

- 1 cup dry bread crumbs
- 2 medium garlic cloves, coarsely chopped
- 1 small onion, quartered
- 6 ounces ground beef
- 6 ounces ground pork
- 2 eggs
- ½ cup grated Parmesan cheese
- 2 tablespoons chopped fresh parsley
- 2 teaspoons dried oregano
- 1 teaspoon dried basil
- ¾ teaspoon salt
- ½ cup olive oil

TOMATO SAUCE

- 3 cups beef broth
- 1 28-ounce can whole tomatoes
- 2 tablespoons double-concentrate tomato paste
- 1½ teaspoons dried oregano
- 1½ teaspoons dried basil
- 1½ teaspoons dried marjoram
- 1½ teaspoons sugar

In a food processor fitted with the metal blade, process the bread crumbs, garlic, and onion until finely chopped. Add the beef, pork, eggs, Parmesan cheese, herbs, and salt. Process until well blended.

In a large skillet, heat the olive oil over moderate-to-high heat. Moisten your hands and shape the mixture into 1½-inch meatballs, carefully adding them to the skillet without overcrowding. Sauté until meatballs are evenly browned, about 5 minutes. Pour off the fat from the skillet.

Add the broth to the skillet and gently boil. Stir and scrape the bottom of the pan with a slotted spoon to dissolve the pan deposits. Add the tomatoes, breaking them apart with your hands. Stir in remaining ingredients. Return the meatballs to the skillet and gently boil until the sauce is thick, 15 to 20 minutes. Serve over cooked pasta.

Serves 4–6

LAMB MEATBALLS WITH RED LENTILS

There's a decidedly Middle Eastern accent to this topping. Red lentils are sometimes called orange or pink lentils. If you can't find them, substitute brown or green ones. Serve over robust pastas such as spaghetti, medium-to-broad ribbons, penne, or shells.

LAMB MEATBALLS

- 1 cup coarse bread crumbs
- 4 garlic cloves, coarsely chopped
- 1 1-by-1-inch piece fresh ginger, peeled and coarsely chopped
- ½ pound ground lamb
- 2 eggs
- ¼ cup parsley leaves
- ½ teaspoon salt
- ½ teaspoon freshly ground black pepper
- 4-6 tablespoons olive oil

RED LENTIL SAUCE

- 1½ tablespoons olive oil
- 2 medium garlic cloves, finely chopped
- 1 medium onion, finely chopped
- ¾ teaspoon ground cumin
- ¾ teaspoon ground coriander seed
- 2 cups beef broth
- ¾ cup red lentils, cleaned and sorted
- 1 14½-ounce can whole tomatoes
- 1 teaspoon dried oregano
- ¾ teaspoon sugar
- ½ teaspoon crushed red pepper flakes
- ½ teaspoon salt

In a food processor fitted with the metal blade, process the bread crumbs, garlic, and ginger until finely chopped. Add the lamb, eggs, parsley, salt, and black pepper; process until smooth.

In a large skillet, heat 4 tablespoons of the oil over moderate heat. Moisten your hands and shape the lamb mixture into 1-inch balls. As you do so, carefully place them in the skillet, taking care not to overcrowd them. Fry the meatballs for about 5 minutes, until evenly browned, adding more oil if necessary. Remove them from the skillet and drain them on paper towels. Drain the skillet and wipe it clean.

For the sauce, heat the olive oil over moderate heat. Add the garlic and onion; sauté until tender, 2 to 3 minutes. Add the cumin and coriander; sauté about 30 seconds more. Then add the broth and raise the heat slightly.

When the broth begins to simmer, add the lentils and then the tomatoes, breaking them up with your hands. Stir in the remaining ingredients, reduce the heat and gently boil until the lentils are tender, 20 to 25 minutes. Add a little water if the lentils cook too dry. During the last 10 minutes of cooking, add the meatballs to the sauce so they cook through. Serve over cooked pasta.

Serves 4-6

3
VEGETABLE SAUCES

QUICK FRESH TOMATO WITH BASIL

MARINARA

CALABRESE-STYLE TOMATO WITH GINGER

MUSHROOM-TOMATO

TOMATO-ANCHOVY

COLD TOMATO WITH RICOTTA

RATATOUILLE

TOMATO PRIMAVERA

CREAMY PARMESAN PRIMAVERA

OLIVE OIL PRIMAVERA SAUTE

SIZZLED SCALLIONS, GARLIC, AND RED CHILI

ASPARAGUS SAUTE WITH BUTTER AND GARLIC

BABY ARTICHOKE HEARTS, GARLIC, AND OLIVE OIL

BROCCOLI WITH OLIVE OIL AND BROWNED GARLIC

MUSHROOM-GARLIC

ZUCCHINI SAUTE WITH BASIL

MIXED BELL PEPPER SAUTE

RED AND YELLOW CHERRY TOMATO SAUTE

FRIZZLED SPINACH WITH PROSCIUTTO

PEAS WITH PROSCIUTTO

PEAS WITH HAM IN CREAM

LEEK CREAM WITH BACON

BROCCOLI WITH GOAT CHEESE

GOLDEN ONION

CLASSIC BASIL PESTO

SPINACH-WALNUT PESTO

PARSLEY-HAZELNUT PESTO

SUN-DRIED TOMATO PESTO

RED BELL PEPPER PESTO

TAPENADE

QUICK FRESH TOMATO
WITH BASIL

Make this sauce in high summer, when the best sun-ripened fresh plum or Roma tomatoes are in season. Serve with fine-to-medium strands of pasta such as angel hair or spaghetti.

1⅔ **pounds Roma tomatoes**
¼ **cup olive oil**
4 **medium garlic cloves, finely chopped**
½ **cup packed finely shredded fresh basil leaves**
1½ **teaspoons dried oregano**
1 **teaspoon salt**

Bring a large saucepan of water to a boil. With a small, sharp knife, remove the core of each tomato and lightly score its skin into four segments. Put the tomatoes in the water and parboil for 30 seconds, then lift them out with a slotted spoon.

When the tomatoes are cool enough to handle, peel off their skins. Cut each in half horizontally and, with your finger or the handle of a teaspoon, scoop out and discard the seeds. Coarsely chop the tomato pulp.

In a large skillet, heat the olive oil over moderate heat. Add the garlic and sauté for about 1 minute. Add the tomatoes, raise the heat, and sauté them just until their juices thicken, about 5 minutes.

Add the herbs and salt; simmer about 1 minute more. Pour over cooked pasta.

Serves 4–6

MARINARA

This classic, quick tomato sauce can be made any time of year with canned tomatoes. Serve with angel hair pasta or spaghettini.

>   3 tablespoons olive oil
>   3 large shallots, finely chopped
>   3 medium garlic cloves, finely chopped
>   1 28-ounce can whole tomatoes
>   6 large basil leaves, finely chopped
>   2 bay leaves
>   1 tablespoon double-concentrate tomato paste
>   1 tablespoon sugar
> 1½ teaspoons dried oregano
>   1 teaspoon dried marjoram
>   ¾ teaspoon salt

In a medium skillet or saucepan, heat the oil over moderate heat. Add the shallots and garlic; sauté until tender, 2 to 3 minutes. Add the tomatoes, breaking them up with your hands. Stir in remaining ingredients.

Raise the heat slightly and simmer the sauce until thick, about 15 minutes. Remove the bay leaves and pour the sauce over cooked pasta.

Serves 4–6

CALABRESE-STYLE TOMATO WITH GINGER

In the Calabrese region of southern Italy, the natives often add ginger to their sauces. It enhances the flavor of the tomatoes and gives the sauce an extra zing. Serve with large shells or tube pastas.

- 3 tablespoons vegetable oil
- 2 medium garlic cloves, finely chopped
- 1 small onion, finely chopped
- 2 teaspoons finely chopped fresh ginger
- 1 28-ounce can whole tomatoes
- 1 tablespoon double-concentrate tomato paste
- 2 teaspoons sugar
- 1 teaspoon dried oregano
- 1 teaspoon dried basil
- ¾ teaspoon salt
- ½ teaspoon freshly ground black pepper

In a medium skillet or saucepan, heat the oil over moderate heat. Add the garlic, onion, and ginger; sauté until tender, 2 to 3 minutes. Add the tomatoes, breaking them apart with your hands. Stir in remaining ingredients.

Raise the heat slightly and simmer the sauce until thick, about 15 minutes. Pour the sauce over cooked pasta.

Serves 4–6

MUSHROOM-TOMATO

In this sauce, ordinary button mushrooms blend perfectly with tomatoes and a healthy dose of garlic. Serve with spaghetti or medium pasta shells.

- 6 tablespoons olive oil
- 6 medium garlic cloves, finely chopped
- 1½ pounds button mushrooms, cut into ¼-inch-thick slices
- 1 28-ounce can whole tomatoes
- 1½ tablespoons chopped fresh parsley
- 1 tablespoon double-concentrate tomato paste
- 1½ teaspoons sugar
- ¾ teaspoon salt

In a large skillet, heat the oil over moderate heat. Add the garlic and sauté until tender, about 2 minutes. Add the mushrooms and raise the heat to high. Sauté the mushrooms until they wilt and begin to brown around the edges, 7 to 10 minutes.

Add the tomatoes, breaking them apart with your hands. Stir in remaining ingredients. Simmer the sauce until thick, about 15 minutes. Pour the sauce over cooked pasta.

Serves 4–6

TOMATO-ANCHOVY

Offer this sauce to confirmed anchovy-haters and defy them to tell you what's in it. The anchovies dissolve during cooking and become a distinctive yet subtle seasoning to what is basically a light tomato-garlic sauce. If you're a real anchovy lover, you can add twice as many fillets.

Serve with spaghetti, linguini, or medium pasta shells.

2 tablespoons olive oil
3 medium garlic cloves, coarsely chopped
1 2-ounce tin anchovy fillets, drained and finely chopped
1 28-ounce can whole tomatoes
1 teaspoon sugar
½ cup coarsely chopped fresh parsley
Freshly ground black pepper

In a medium saucepan, heat the olive oil over moderate heat. Add the garlic and sauté until tender, 2 to 3 minutes. Add the anchovy fillets, tomatoes, and sugar; raise the heat slightly to bring the liquid to a gentle boil as you stir occasionally, breaking up the tomatoes.

Reduce the heat and simmer the sauce until thick, about 15 minutes. Stir in the parsley and pour over cooked pasta. Season with black pepper to taste.

Serves 4-6

COLD TOMATO WITH RICOTTA

During the heat of the summer, when fresh Roma tomatoes are in season, make this simple yet flavorful cold sauce. Toss it with angel hair pasta or spaghetti.

1 pound Roma tomatoes
¾ pound fresh ricotta cheese, crumbled
4 medium garlic cloves, finely chopped
⅓ cup packed finely shredded fresh basil leaves
6 tablespoons lemon juice
¼ cup olive oil
2 teaspoons salt
2 teaspoons freshly ground white pepper
1 teaspoon sugar

Bring a large saucepan of water to a boil. With a small, sharp knife, remove the core of each tomato and lightly score its skin into four segments. Put the tomatoes in the water and parboil for 30 seconds, then lift them out with a slotted spoon.

When the tomatoes are cool enough to handle, peel off their skins. Cut each in half horizontally and, with your finger or the handle of a teaspoon, scoop out and discard the seeds. Coarsely chop the tomato pulp.

In a large serving bowl, combine the tomatoes with the remaining ingredients, stirring thoroughly, but gently, to avoid mashing the tomatoes or ricotta.

Let the sauce sit at room temperature while you cook the pasta. Add the hot drained pasta to the serving bowl and toss well to mix it with the sauce. Serve immediately.

Serves 4-6

RATATOUILLE

In this recipe, I've adapted the classic southern French cooked vegetable mixture to make a quick, chunky sauce. Serve it with broad pasta ribbons or large pasta shells.

3 tablespoons olive oil

1 medium onion, coarsely chopped

1 large garlic clove, coarsely chopped

¾ pound Roma tomatoes, stemmed and coarsely chopped

¼ pound eggplant, peeled and cut into ½-inch cubes

¼ pound zucchini, trimmed and cut into ½-inch cubes

1 small green bell pepper, stemmed, seeded, and cut into ½-inch pieces

1 tablespoon double-concentrate tomato paste

1 teaspoon dried oregano

1 teaspoon dried basil

1 teaspoon sugar

1 teaspoon salt

In a large saucepan, heat the oil over moderate heat. Add the onion and garlic; sauté until tender, about 3 minutes.

Add the vegetables. Sauté them for a few minutes, until they begin to exude their juices.

Stir in the remaining ingredients. Simmer the sauce until the vegetables are tender-crisp, about 15 minutes. Spoon over cooked pasta.

Serves 4–6

TOMATO PRIMAVERA

Primavera is Italian for "springtime." The term generally refers to any sauce full of fresh, seasonal vegetables. Here, they are in a tomato-based sauce. Feel free to vary the vegetables by adding what's best in the market.

Serve with spaghetti, linguini, fettuccine, or other medium strands or medium ribbons of pasta.

- 1 tablespoon olive oil
- 1 small onion, finely chopped
- 1 large garlic clove, finely chopped
- 1 14½-ounce can whole tomatoes
- 1 small ear corn, kernels shucked and parboiled for 1 minute
- 1 small zucchini, cut into ¼-inch cubes
- 1 small golden squash, cut into ¼-inch cubes
- 1 small carrot, cut into ¼-inch cubes
- 2 ounces extra-small button mushrooms, halved
- 1 teaspoon double-concentrate tomato paste
- ¾ teaspoon dried oregano
- ½ teaspoon dried basil
- ½ teaspoon sugar
- ½ teaspoon salt

In a large skillet or saucepan, heat the oil over moderate heat. Add the onion and garlic; sauté until tender, 2 to 3 minutes.

Add the tomatoes, breaking them up with your hands. Stir in remaining ingredients. Raise the heat slightly and simmer the sauce until thick, about 10 minutes. Spoon over cooked pasta.

Serves 4–6

CREAMY PARMESAN PRIMAVERA

This version of a primavera sauce enrobes the vegetables in a white wine cream sauce made with plenty of Parmesan cheese. Serve with medium strands or tubes of pasta such as spaghetti, tagliatelli, linguini, or penne.

- ¼ cup unsalted butter
- 2 medium shallots, finely chopped
- 1 medium garlic clove, finely chopped
- 2 small carrots, cut diagonally into ⅛-inch-thick slices
- 2 small zucchini, cut diagonally into ⅛-inch-thick slices
- ½ pound peas, shelled
- 6 ounces button mushrooms, cut into ¼-inch-thick slices
- 1 cup dry white wine
- 2 cups heavy cream
- ½ cup grated Parmesan cheese
- 2 tablespoons chopped fresh parsley
- ½ teaspoon salt
- ½ teaspoon freshly ground white pepper
- Dash nutmeg

In a large skillet, melt the butter over moderate heat. Add the shallots and garlic; sauté for about 1 minute. Raise the heat to high and add all the vegetables; sauté for 2 to 3 minutes. Remove them from the skillet and set aside.

Add the wine to the skillet. Bring it to a brisk boil and continue boiling until it is reduced by half, 5 to 7 minutes. Add the cream and gently boil until the liquid is thick, 7 to 10 minutes more.

Stir in the sautéed vegetables and simmer until just heated through, 2 to 3 minutes more. Stir in the Parmesan cheese, parsley, and seasonings. Pour immediately over cooked pasta.

Serves 4–6

OLIVE OIL PRIMAVERA SAUTE

This is the simplest of fresh spring vegetable toppings. Its quality depends upon the quality of the ingredients you use. Choose the best, fruitiest, fullest-flavored olive oil; the freshest vegetables; and a good, sharp Parmesan cheese.
Serve with angel hair or other delicate strands of pasta.

¾ **cup olive oil**
3 **medium garlic cloves, unpeeled and smashed**
½ **pound small snow peas, trimmed**
⅓ **pound extra-small button mushrooms (if larger, cut into ¼-inch-thick slices)**
2 **small carrots, cut diagonally into ⅛-inch-thick slices**
2 **small zucchini, cut diagonally into ⅛-inch-thick slices**
1 **medium red bell pepper, stemmed, seeded, quartered, and cut crosswise into ¼-inch-thick slices**
1½ **tablespoons chopped fresh parsley**
1 **teaspoon salt**
Freshly ground black pepper
Grated Parmesan cheese

In a large skillet or wok, heat the olive oil with the garlic over moderate heat. Remove and discard the garlic as soon as it turns golden, after about 3 minutes.

Raise the heat, add the vegetables, and sauté or stir-fry them until hot, but still very crisp, about 1 minute. Immediately spoon or pour the vegetables and oil over cooked pasta.

With a fork, quickly arrange the vegetables into a decorative pattern, if you like. Sprinkle with parsley, salt, and black pepper. Let each guest add plenty of Parmesan cheese to taste.

Serves 4–6

SIZZLED SCALLIONS, GARLIC, AND RED CHILI

East meets West in this simple topping for which you stir-fry slivered scallions and hot red chili flakes Szechuan-style in good Italian olive oil. Serve it over spaghetti, other medium pasta strands, or Chinese egg noodles.

- 1¼ **cups olive oil**
- 8 **medium scallions, trimmed, cut into 1-inch sections, then cut lengthwise into slivers**
- 4 **medium garlic cloves, finely chopped**
- 4 **teaspoons crushed red pepper flakes**
- 1 **teaspoon salt**

In a large skillet or wok, heat the oil over moderate-to-high heat. Add all the remaining ingredients and stir-fry until the scallions are slightly scorched, about 1 minute. Pour immediately over cooked pasta.

Serves 4–6

ASPARAGUS SAUTE WITH BUTTER AND GARLIC

Springtime's earliest asparagus is so thin, tender, and sweet that it needs only the simplest treatment to become a perfect topping for pasta. Serve with thin, delicate pasta such as angel hair.

1¼ cups (2½ sticks) unsalted butter, cut into pieces
4 large garlic cloves, finely chopped
36 thin asparagus spears, ends trimmed, cut diagonally into ¼-inch-thick slices (about 3 cups)
1 lemon, cut into wedges
Salt and freshly ground black pepper
Grated Parmesan cheese

In a large skillet, melt the butter over high heat. As soon as it foams, add the garlic and sauté until it turns light golden, about 1 minute.

Add the asparagus and sauté until it is tender-crisp and the garlic is nicely browned, 4 to 5 minutes.

Serve immediately over cooked pasta. Let each guest add a squeeze of lemon, salt, and black pepper to taste, and plenty of Parmesan.

Serves 4-6

BABY ARTICHOKE HEARTS, GARLIC, AND OLIVE OIL

Watch your market or produce store for one of spring and summer's best treats: baby artichokes, hardly bigger than a jumbo egg. It's an easy task to strip the leaves from them and pare off their skins, leaving the tender baby artichoke hearts. Olive oil and garlic are logical partners for this quick, fresh pasta topping.

Serve with medium ribbons of pasta such as fettuccine, or with medium pasta shapes such as bow ties or shells.

> 1¼ **cups olive oil**
> 6 **medium garlic cloves, cut lengthwise into thin slivers**
> 2 **pounds baby artichokes, stemmed, pared, and quartered**
> **Salt and freshly ground black pepper**
> **Grated Parmesan cheese**

In a large skillet, heat the oil with the garlic over moderate-to-high heat, until the garlic turns a light golden color, 2 to 3 minutes.

Add the artichoke hearts, reduce the heat slightly, and sauté them until they are golden brown, 5 to 7 minutes more. Serve immediately over pasta. Season to taste with salt, black pepper, and Parmesan.

Serves 4–6

BROCCOLI WITH OLIVE OIL AND BROWNED GARLIC

Broccoli and garlic are natural partners, especially when bound by a good olive oil. Serve with spaghetti or thin-to-medium pasta tubes such as bucatini or penne.

1¼ cups olive oil
6 medium garlic cloves, sliced thin lengthwise
2½ pounds broccoli, cut into ¾-inch florets
Salt and freshly ground black pepper
Grated Parmesan cheese

In a large skillet, heat the olive oil and garlic over moderate-to-high heat until the garlic turns a light golden color, 2 to 3 minutes. Add the broccoli and sauté until it is dark green and tender-crisp, about 3 minutes.

Immediately spoon the broccoli, garlic, and oil over cooked pasta. Season to taste with salt, black pepper, and Parmesan cheese.

Serves 4-6

MUSHROOM-GARLIC

This is definitely a sauce for garlic lovers (not to mention lovers of mushrooms). It may seem like a large quantity of mushrooms to use, but once their liquid evaporates, you'll have just the right amount.

Serve with medium strands of pasta such as spaghetti or linguini. This sauce also goes well with medium shells or other pasta shapes.

- 1 cup (2 sticks) unsalted butter, cut into pieces
- 8 medium garlic cloves, finely chopped
- 3 pounds button mushrooms, cut into ¼-inch-thick slices (if large, cut in half before slicing crosswise)
- 6 tablespoons heavy cream
- 6 tablespoons chopped fresh parsley
- Salt and freshly ground white pepper
- Grated Parmesan cheese

In a large skillet, melt the butter over moderate-to-high heat. Add the garlic and sauté for about 1 minute.

Add the mushrooms and stir well to coat them with the hot butter. As the mushroom slices begin to exude liquid, raise the heat slightly. Sauté, stirring frequently, until only a few tablespoons of liquid remain, 20 to 25 minutes.

Stir in the cream and parsley; simmer until the liquid has reduced to a thick coating consistency, 3 to 5 minutes more. Season to taste with salt and white pepper; pour immediately over cooked pasta. Add Parmesan cheese to taste.

Serves 4-6

ZUCCHINI SAUTE WITH BASIL

If you shred and salt zucchini, it cooks up crisply—a real surprise to those who ordinarily dislike this vegetable. Served over angel hair, spaghetti, or other thin-to-medium pasta strands, the zucchini provides an interesting counterpoint of texture and flavor.

> 2 pounds medium zucchini
> 2 teaspoons salt
> ⅓ cup packed finely shredded fresh basil leaves
> 1¼ cups olive oil
> 4 medium garlic cloves, finely chopped
> Freshly ground black pepper
> Grated Parmesan cheese

Using a food processor or hand grater, finely shred the zucchini. In a mixing bowl, toss the zucchini shreds with the salt, mixing them well. Let them stand for about 10 minutes. Then pick up small handfuls of zucchini and, working over the sink, squeeze the zucchini tightly to extract as much liquid as possible. (Much of the salt will go down the drain with the liquid.)

Put the squeezed zucchini shreds in another bowl and toss them with the shredded basil.

In a large skillet, heat the olive oil with the garlic over moderate-to-high heat. As soon as the garlic sizzles, add the zucchini-basil mixture and sauté just until the shreds begin to turn golden, about 4 minutes.

Spoon the vegetables and oil over cooked pasta and add plenty of black pepper and Parmesan cheese.

Serves 4-6

MIXED BELL PEPPER SAUTE

At the height of summer, good produce departments carry a bright array of bell peppers—green, red, yellow, orange, purple-black. I love to combine as many different colors as possible to make a quick pepper strip sauté.

A lot of peppers go into this recipe; if your skillet isn't big enough, you may want to cook it in two batches. Serve over fettuccine or other medium ribbons of pasta.

$1\frac{1}{4}$ cups olive oil
 8 medium bell peppers in assorted colors, halved, stemmed, seeded, and cut crosswise into $\frac{1}{4}$-inch strips (about 9 cups packed loose)
 6 medium garlic cloves, finely chopped
 6 tablespoons chopped fresh parsley
 3 tablespoons lemon juice
$1\frac{1}{2}$ teaspoons salt
 $\frac{3}{4}$ teaspoon freshly ground black pepper

In a large skillet, heat the olive oil over moderate-to-high heat. Add the bell peppers and sauté until tender, 7 to 10 minutes (they will reduce considerably in volume).

Add the garlic and sauté just until you can smell its aroma, about 30 seconds; then stir in the parsley, lemon juice, salt, and black pepper. Serve immediately over cooked pasta.

Serves 4-6

RED AND YELLOW CHERRY TOMATO SAUTE

In the late spring and summer, you'll find wonderful cherry tomatoes in the supermarket. Many good greengrocers now carry beautiful golden cherry tomatoes as well as the familiar red variety. Their flavors are similar (and you can certainly use all red if you can't find yellow), but together they make a vibrantly pretty topping for pasta.

Depending on the size of your skillet, cook the tomatoes in two to four batches for best results. Serve with angel hair, spaghettini, or other fine pasta strands.

    1¼ **cups olive oil**
    6 **garlic cloves, finely chopped**
  60 **red cherry tomatoes, halved**
  60 **yellow cherry tomatoes, halved**
    ¼ **cup chopped fresh parsley**
    2 **tablespoons chopped fresh chives**

In a large skillet, heat the olive oil over moderate-to-high heat. Add the garlic and sauté for about 30 seconds. Then add the cherry tomatoes.

Sauté the tomatoes until their skins shrivel and they are heated through. Toss with the parsley and chives. Pour immediately over cooked pasta.

Serves 4–6

FRIZZLED SPINACH WITH PROSCIUTTO

Raw spinach, thrown into hot olive oil, frizzles. It gets a crisp-tender texture and an intense flavor that, to my mind, is the most delicious way to enjoy this vegetable.

Combined with thin strips of crisply fried prosciutto, garlic, and a pinch of crushed red pepper flakes, it makes a quick, simple pasta topping.

Serve over spaghetti, linguini, or other medium pasta strands.

$1\frac{1}{4}$ cups olive oil
6 medium garlic cloves, finely chopped
$\frac{1}{2}$ pound thinly sliced prosciutto, cut into $\frac{1}{4}$-inch-wide strips
2 bunches spinach, stemmed, ribbed, thoroughly washed, and leaves cut crosswise into $\frac{1}{4}$-inch-wide strips
2 teaspoons crushed red pepper flakes
Freshly ground black pepper

In a large skillet, heat the oil over moderate-to-high heat. Add the garlic and sauté for about 1 minute. Then add the prosciutto and sauté until it begins to frizzle, 2 to 3 minutes more.

Add the spinach leaves and the pepper flakes to the oil; stir quickly until all the shreds have frizzled, about 30 seconds. Spoon immediately over cooked pasta and season generously with black pepper.

Serves 4–6

PEAS WITH PROSCIUTTO

Thin strips of prosciutto make a classic Italian accompaniment to peas. This recipe joins them in a quick butter sauce.

Serve over medium ribbons of pasta such as tagliatelli or fettuccine or serve with small-to-medium pasta shapes such as shells or bow ties.

- 1¼ **cups (2½ sticks) unsalted butter, cut into pieces**
- 6 **tablespoons olive oil**
- 4 **medium garlic cloves, finely chopped**
- ⅓ **pound thinly sliced prosciutto, cut into ¼-inch-wide strips**
- 3 **pounds peas, shelled and parboiled for 2 to 3 minutes**
- 6 **tablespoons chopped fresh parsley**
- **Freshly ground black pepper**
- **Grated Parmesan cheese**

In a large skillet, melt the butter with the oil over moderate-to-high heat. Add the garlic and prosciutto; sauté until the prosciutto begins to frizzle, 2 to 3 minutes.

Add the peas and parsley; sauté until the peas are heated through, about 1 minute more. Serve immediately over cooked pasta. Season generously with black pepper and Parmesan cheese.

Serves 4–6

PEAS WITH HAM IN CREAM

In this topping, strips of smoky Black Forest ham and a rich sauce of cream and Parmesan cheese provide the perfect accompaniment for fresh garden peas. Serve over elbow macaroni, small shells, or other small-to-medium shaped pastas.

- **3 tablespoons unsalted butter**
- **⅓ pound sliced Black Forest ham, cut into strips ¼-inch wide by 1 to 2 inches long**
- **2 cups heavy cream**
- **1½ pounds peas, shelled and parboiled for 2 to 3 minutes**
- **1½ cups grated Parmesan cheese**
- **Salt and freshly ground black pepper**

In a large skillet, melt the butter over moderate heat. Add the ham and sauté until lightly browned, 3 to 5 minutes. Remove the ham strips and set them aside to drain on paper towels; pour off all but a thin film of fat from the skillet.

Add the cream to the skillet, raise the heat and bring it to a boil; gently boil, stirring and scraping the bottom of the pan with a wooden spoon to dissolve the pan deposits. Continue cooking until the cream has reduced by about ½ cup, about 15 minutes.

Add the peas and ham; stir in the Parmesan cheese. Reduce the heat and simmer for 2 to 3 minutes more. Season with salt and black pepper to taste and serve immediately over cooked pasta.

Serves 4-6

LEEK CREAM WITH BACON

Leeks have a mild, sweet oniony flavor that goes excellently with cream and a subtle touch of bacon to make a fine topping for spaghetti, linguini, or other medium strands of pasta.

10 tablespoons (1¼ sticks) unsalted butter, cut into pieces
2 strips bacon, cut crosswise into ¼-inch-wide strips
5 medium leeks, trimmed, split lengthwise, washed thoroughly, and cut into ¼-inch-thick slices
4 medium shallots, thinly sliced
4 medium garlic cloves, finely chopped
2½ cups heavy cream
1¼ cups chicken broth
½ teaspoon salt
¼ cup chopped fresh chervil or parsley

In a large skillet, melt the butter over moderate heat. Add the bacon and sauté for 2 to 3 minutes. Add the leeks, shallots, and garlic; sauté for 2 to 3 minutes more, until the vegetables just soften.

Stir in the cream, broth, and salt. Raise the heat and bring the sauce to a boil. Gently boil until the sauce is thick and creamy, 20 to 25 minutes. Stir in the chervil or parsley before pouring over cooked pasta.

Serves 4–6

BROCCOLI WITH GOAT CHEESE

This is one of those culinary miracles where two pungent-smelling and strong-flavored ingredients marry into an exquisite dish. Serve over fettuccine or other medium-to-wide noodles or with medium-to-large pasta shells.

- ¾ cup (1½ sticks) unsalted butter, cut into pieces
- 6 cups packed broccoli florets, parboiled until tender-crisp, about 30 seconds
- 1 pound creamy goat cheese, cut into pieces
- Salt and freshly ground black pepper

In a large skillet, melt the butter over moderate heat. Add the broccoli florets and toss them until thoroughly coated with butter and heated through, about 2 minutes.

Add the goat cheese; stir until it melts and coats the broccoli. Immediately pour the sauce over cooked pasta. Season with salt and plenty of black pepper to taste.

Serves 4–6

GOLDEN ONION

Cooked slowly in butter, onions develop a deep caramel color and intense sweetness that are showcased in this sauce for onion-lovers. For extra sweetness, use Walla Walla, Vidalia, or Maui onions.

Even those who aren't too wild about onions will enjoy this sauce on a pasta side dish served with roast beef or lamb.

Serve over spaghetti or other medium strands of pasta.

1 cup (2 sticks) unsalted butter, cut into pieces
1¾ pounds sweet yellow onions, thinly sliced
2 teaspoons sugar
1½ teaspoons salt
1¾ cups heavy cream
6 tablespoons chopped fresh chives
Freshly ground black pepper
Grated Parmesan cheese

In a large skillet or saucepan, melt the butter over moderate-to-low heat. Add the onions, sugar, and salt; cook, stirring occasionally, until all the liquid exuded by the onions evaporates, about 10 minutes.

Reduce the heat slightly and continue cooking, stirring occasionally, until the onions reduce to a caramel-colored paste, about 20 minutes more.

Stir in the cream and simmer briefly until it is absorbed by the onions. Stir in the chives and serve immediately over cooked pasta with generous amounts of black pepper and Parmesan cheese.

Serves 4–6

CLASSIC BASIL PESTO

It's almost impossible to heap too much praise upon this sauce from the northwestern Italian city of Genoa. An uncooked puree of fresh basil, pine nuts, garlic, olive oil, and Parmesan cheese, pesto has an incredibly heady aroma and flavor, and a truly voluptuous consistency.

Serve it over delicate-to-medium strands or ribbons of pasta—angel hair, spaghetti, linguini, tagliatelli, fettuccine.

- ¾ **cup pine nuts**
- 3 **cups packed stemmed fresh basil leaves**
- 1½ **cups olive oil**
- 1 **cup grated Parmesan cheese**
- 4 **medium garlic cloves**

Spread the pine nuts on a baking sheet and toast them in a 450°F oven until golden brown, about 10 minutes; watch them carefully to guard against burning.

Put all the ingredients into a food processor fitted with the metal blade. Turning the machine on and off rapidly, pulse the ingredients several times until coarsely chopped. Scrape down the work bowl. Then process continuously until the sauce is smooth. If the pesto seems too thick, pulse in a little hot water.

Toss with cooked pasta the moment the pasta has been drained.

Serves 4–6

SPINACH-WALNUT PESTO

This variation on the classic recipe has an intense green color and a flavor as bold as the original. Serve over delicate-to-medium strands or ribbons of pasta.

- 1¼ cups packed, stemmed, and ribbed spinach leaves, thoroughly washed
- 1 cup olive oil
- 1 cup grated Romano cheese
- 1 cup shelled walnut pieces
- 2 medium garlic cloves
- 2 tablespoons lemon juice
- ¾ teaspoon salt

Put all the ingredients into a food processor fitted with the metal blade. Turning the machine on and off rapidly, pulse the ingredients several times until coarsely chopped. Scrape down the work bowl. Then process continuously until the sauce is smooth. If the pesto seems too thick, pulse in a little hot water.

Toss with cooked pasta the moment the pasta has been drained.

Serves 4–6

PARSLEY-HAZELNUT PESTO

A lot of pesto recipes economize on basil by substituting parsley for half of it. I prefer to keep the parsley out of the original recipe and use it, instead, in this unique variation.

Serve over delicate-to-medium strands or ribbons of pasta.

- ¾ **cup hazelnuts**
- 1¾ **cups packed fresh parsley leaves**
- ½ **cup plus 2 tablespoons walnut oil**
- ½ **cup plus 2 tablespoons corn or peanut oil**
- 1¼ **cups grated Romano cheese**
- 2 **medium garlic cloves**

Spread the hazelnuts on a baking sheet and toast them in a 400°F oven, 10 to 15 minutes. When they're cool enough to handle, rub the skins off the nuts.

Put all the ingredients into a food processor fitted with the metal blade. Turning the machine on and off rapidly, pulse the ingredients several times until coarsely chopped. Scrape down the work bowl. Then process continuously until the sauce is smooth. If the pesto seems too thick, pulse in a little hot water.

Toss with cooked pasta the moment the pasta has been drained.

Serves 4–6

SUN-DRIED TOMATO PESTO

This has become as much a favorite of mine as the classic basil version. Most gourmet markets now carry sun-dried tomatoes packed in olive oil. They keep well and are worth buying in quantity.

Serve over delicate-to-medium strands or ribbons of pasta.

- **3 cups packed drained sun-dried tomatoes**
- **1½ cups olive oil (you can substitute some of the oil from the tomatoes)**
- **1 cup plus 2 tablespoons grated Parmesan cheese**
- **¾ cup shelled walnut pieces**
- **½ cup packed fresh parsley leaves**
- **3 medium garlic cloves**

Put all the ingredients into a food processor fitted with the metal blade. Turning the machine on and off rapidly, pulse the ingredients several times until coarsely chopped. Scrape down the work bowl. Then process continuously until the sauce is smooth. If the pesto seems too thick, pulse in a little hot water.

Toss with cooked pasta the moment the pasta has been drained.

Serves 4–6

RED BELL PEPPER PESTO

When red bell peppers are at their cheapest, try them roasted and pureed in this sweet, sublime pesto variation. You can also use canned, Italian roasted sweet peppers.

Serve over delicate-to-medium strands or ribbons of pasta.

3 **medium red bell peppers, roasted, peeled, stemmed, and seeded**
2 **medium garlic cloves**
1 **cup plus 2 tablespoons olive oil**
¾ **cup whole pitted black olives**
½ **cup grated Parmesan cheese**
½ **cup packed fresh parsley leaves**
3 **tablespoons lemon juice**
1 **teaspoon salt**

Put all the ingredients into a food processor fitted with the metal blade. Turning the machine on and off rapidly, pulse the ingredients several times until coarsely chopped. Scrape down the work bowl. Then process continuously until the sauce is smooth. If the pesto seems too thick, pulse in a little hot water.

Toss with cooked pasta the moment the pasta has been drained.

Serves 4–6

TAPENADE

This pungent paste of olives, garlic, and anchovies is a favorite in Provence, where it is used as a dip or a spread for bread crusts. Thinned with a little extra oil, it makes a great pasta topping.

Serve with spaghetti, linguini, or other medium strands of pasta.

- 1 cup olive oil
- 1 pound medium cured Mediterranean olives, pitted (about 2 cups)
- 3 large garlic cloves
- ¾ cup packed fresh parsley leaves
- 3 2-ounce tins anchovy fillets, drained
- 4½ tablespoons drained capers
- 3 tablespoons lemon juice

Put all the ingredients into a food processor fitted with the metal blade. Turning the machine on and off rapidly, pulse the ingredients several times until coarsely chopped. Scrape down the work bowl. Then process continuously until the sauce is smooth. If the tapenade seems too thick, pulse in a little hot water.

Toss with cooked pasta the moment the pasta has been drained.

Serves 4–6

4

CREAM AND CHEESE SAUCES

RICOTTA AND BUTTER

GARLIC GOAT CHEESE

BOURSIN, FRESH CHIVES, AND PARSLEY

COTTAGE CHEESE, CARAWAY SEEDS,
POPPY SEEDS, AND PAPRIKA

ALFREDO

GORGONZOLA AND PINE NUTS

STILTON, PORT, AND WALNUTS

SPICY CHEDDAR WITH BACON
MASCARPONE AND PANCETTA
FOUR CHEESES
MIMOSA WITH SMOKED MOZZARELLA
AVOCADO–PARMESAN CHEESE
JALAPEÑO CREAM
PORCINI-COGNAC CREAM

RICOTTA AND BUTTER

With its fluffy, smooth texture and creamy flavor, fresh ricotta cheese with melted butter makes a luxurious yet homey and satisfying topping for pasta. Try to buy freshly made ricotta at your local Italian deli; it has a lighter texture and finer flavor than the prepackaged product, although the latter is fine for this dish.

Serve with broad ribbon noodles, medium-sized macaroni, shells, or other shaped pastas. Spinach pasta or other colored pastas contrast nicely with the ricotta.

1 cup (2 sticks) unsalted butter, cut into pieces
2½ pounds ricotta, at room temperature, drained
Salt and freshly ground white pepper
Paprika (optional)

In a medium saucepan or skillet over moderate heat, melt the butter. As soon as it has melted, pour it over the cooked pasta. Roughly crumble the ricotta on top. Season with salt and white pepper to taste, and toss well. If you want to add a touch of color, dust each serving with a little paprika.

Serves 4-6

GARLIC GOAT CHEESE

Creamy fresh goat cheeses are becoming more widely available in cheese stores, gourmet markets, and delis. Use the freshest, creamiest variety you can find. The pungency of the garlic and the bite of the cheese are an excellent combination in this creamy sauce.

Serve over fettuccine or other medium-to-broad noodles. It's also good with medium-sized pasta shapes such as rotelli or bow ties.

> 1 tablespoon unsalted butter
> 3 medium garlic cloves, finely chopped
> 1 cup heavy cream
> ½ pound creamy fresh goat cheese
> Salt and freshly ground white pepper
> 2 tablespoons chopped fresh chives

In a medium skillet, melt the butter over low heat. Add the garlic and sauté until tender, 1 to 2 minutes.

Add the cream, raise the heat to moderate, then stir in the goat cheese until it melts. Season to taste with salt and white pepper. Pour the sauce over cooked pasta and garnish with chives.

Serves 4–6

BOURSIN, FRESH CHIVES, AND PARSLEY

You can make excellent sauces quickly by melting French triple-cream cheeses flavored with garlic and herbs, such as Boursin. Add some chopped fresh herbs and the sauce tastes as good as a cheese-and-cream sauce made entirely from scratch.

Serve over spaghetti, fettuccine, or other medium strands or medium ribbons of pasta.

4 5-ounce packages Boursin cheese with garlic and fines herbes, at room temperature

6 tablespoons chopped fresh chives

6 tablespoons chopped fresh parsley

As soon as the pasta is cooked and drained, dot the cheese on top of it. Scatter on the herbs, and toss well until the cheese has melted and coats the pasta.

Serves 4-6

COTTAGE CHEESE, CARAWAY SEEDS, POPPY SEEDS, AND PAPRIKA

This topping has a decidedly Eastern European influence. It tastes similar to Hungarian liptauer *cheese.*

Serve with broad ribbons of pasta, medium-or-large shells, or other good-sized pasta shapes.

> 1 **quart large-curd cottage cheese, at room temperature**
> ½ **cup poppy seeds**
> ¼ **cup caraway seeds**
> 1 **teaspoon salt**
> **Paprika**

As soon as the pasta is cooked and drained, spoon the cottage cheese on top. Scatter on the seeds and salt; toss thoroughly. Dust generously with paprika.

Serves 4–6

ALFREDO

When served at Alfredo alla Scrofa restaurant in Rome, where it was invented, this sauce is prepared tableside in a chafing dish. But it's easier to make in a saucepan on top of the stove and pour over the pasta on each plate.

Fettuccine is the classic pasta to use, but any ribbons broad enough to hold the creamy sauce will do fine.

> ¾ cup (1½ sticks) unsalted butter, cut into pieces
> 1½ cups heavy cream
> 1¾ cups grated Parmesan cheese
> Freshly ground black pepper

In a medium saucepan, heat the butter and cream over medium heat, stirring occasionally, until the butter melts and the cream is hot.

Gradually stir in 1¼ cups of Parmesan. As soon as the cheese has melted and thickened the sauce, pour the sauce over the cooked pasta. Let guests add more Parmesan to their individual servings and season with black pepper to taste.

Serves 4-6

GORGONZOLA AND PINE NUTS

The creamy Italian blue-veined cheese known as Gorgonzola has a strong, pungent, tangy flavor that ranks it among the world's great cheeses. Toasted pine nuts add an earthy contrast to this rich sauce.

Serve with penne, other tubular pastas, medium-to-broad ribbons, or medium pasta shells.

> 1 cup shelled pine nuts
> 3 cups heavy cream
> 1¾ pounds Gorgonzola cheese, crumbled

Spread the pine nuts on a baking sheet and toast them in a 450°F oven until golden brown, about 10 minutes; watch them carefully to guard against burning.

Meanwhile, put the cream in a medium saucepan and bring it to a boil. Reduce the heat to simmer and add the crumbled Gorgonzola. Stir continuously until the sauce is thick and most of the cheese has melted; some small lumps of cheese should remain.

Pour the sauce over the cooked pasta and scatter the pine nuts generously on top.

Serves 4–6

STILTON, PORT, AND WALNUTS

There's an English air about this sauce, combining as it does the preeminent British blue cheese, Stilton, with its time-honored after-dinner companions, port and walnuts. If you can't get ahold of Stilton, use the creamiest, mellowest blue cheese you can find. The sauce is also excellent with pecans substituted for the walnuts.

Serve with tube pastas such as penne or ziti, or medium-sized pasta shells, or bow ties.

> 1¼ **cups shelled walnuts, broken into pieces**
> 3 **cups heavy cream**
> ¾ **cup port wine**
> 1½ **pounds Stilton cheese, crumbled**

Spread the walnuts on a baking sheet and toast them in a 450°F oven until golden, 5 to 7 minutes.

In a large saucepan, bring the cream to a boil over high heat. Add the port, reduce the heat slightly, and gently boil until reduced by about ½ cup, 7 to 10 minutes. Crumble in the Stilton and continue simmering until it has melted and the sauce is thickened, about 5 minutes more.

Pour the sauce over cooked pasta and scatter the walnuts generously on top.

Serves 4-6

SPICY CHEDDAR WITH BACON

Sharp cheddar is a good foil to hot spices. Think of this sauce as a sort of Welsh rarebit for pasta.

Serve over elbow macaroni or medium-sized pasta shapes such as bow ties or rotelli.

            2 tablespoons unsalted butter
          1¾ pounds sliced bacon, cut into ¼-inch-wide strips
          3½ cups heavy cream
          1¾ pounds sharp cheddar cheese, shredded
            1 teaspoon Dijon-style mustard
            6 drops hot pepper sauce
    Salt and freshly ground black pepper

In a large skillet, melt the butter over moderate heat. Add the bacon and sauté it until crisp, 5 to 7 minutes. Drain the bacon on paper towels, and pour off all but the thinnest film of the fat from the pan.

Add the cream to the skillet and bring it to a boil over moderate heat. Add the cheddar cheese and stir until it melts and thickens the sauce. Stir in the mustard and hot pepper sauce. Add salt and black pepper to taste.

Pour the sauce over cooked pasta, and scatter the bacon on top.

Serves 4–6

MASCARPONE AND PANCETTA

Mascarpone, a specialty of the Lombard region of northern Italy, is one of the most luxurious cheeses in existence. It is a fresh, slightly tangy, buttery double-cream that's just one step beyond heavy cream.

Many gourmet stores and Italian delis now sell it in cartons. It's worth seeking out for this sauce, which combines the cheese with pancetta, a fine, rolled, Italian bacon.

Serve over angel hair, spaghetti, or other fine-to-medium strands of pasta.

> ¼ **cup unsalted butter, cut into pieces**
> ½ **pound thinly sliced pancetta, coarsely chopped**
> 3 **cups Mascarpone**
> **Grated Parmesan cheese**
> **Freshly ground black pepper**

In a large skillet, melt the butter over moderate heat. Add the pancetta and sauté it just until it begins to brown around the edges, about 3 minutes.

Stir in the Mascarpone. As soon as it begins to bubble, pour the sauce over cooked pasta. Season with plenty of Parmesan cheese and black pepper to taste.

Serves 4–6

FOUR CHEESES

The key to this sauce is choosing four cheeses whose flavors and textures complement each other. My choices here are a rich cheddar; a mellow smoked Gouda; a sharp, tangy Swiss Appenzeller; and Parmesan cheese. Have fun selecting your own combination, adding a blue cheese, if you like, or perhaps a mozzarella for the appealing strings it forms when melted.

Serve with short or long tubes of pasta such as macaroni, penne, or ziti.

> 2½ **cups heavy cream**
> ¼ **pound cheddar cheese, shredded**
> ¼ **pound smoked Gouda cheese, shredded**
> ¼ **pound Appenzeller cheese, shredded**
> ½ **cup grated Parmesan cheese**

Put the cream in a medium saucepan over moderate heat. As soon as the cream is hot, but before it starts to boil, stir in the cheeses.

Raise the heat slightly as they begin to melt, and bring the sauce to a boil, stirring constantly. Reduce the heat and simmer gently until the sauce is thick and creamy, about 5 minutes. Pour over cooked pasta and serve immediately.

Serves 4–6

MIMOSA WITH SMOKED MOZZARELLA

In springtime, the branches of the mimosa tree are decked with frothy, pale yellow blossoms. This rich sauce mimics that effect.

Since it requires no cooking, all ingredients must be at room temperature. To make preparation easier, shred the mozzarella while it's still cold.

Serve over spaghetti, linguini, or fettuccine.

- **6 egg yolks, at room temperature**
- **1 cup plus 2 tablespoons heavy cream, at room temperature**
- **¾ cup grated Parmesan cheese**
- **⅔ pound smoked mozzarella cheese, finely shredded and at room temperature**
- **3 tablespoons finely chopped fresh parsley**
- **1 tablespoon finely chopped fresh chives**
- **1 teaspoon salt**
- **1 teaspoon freshly ground black pepper**

In a large pasta serving bowl, beat the egg yolks until smooth; stir in the cream. Add the remaining ingredients and stir well.

The moment the pasta is cooked and drained, add it to the bowl and toss thoroughly, letting the heat of the pasta cook the sauce.

Serves 4–6

AVOCADO-PARMESAN CHEESE

Odd as it may sound, this combination makes a lovely sauce for pastas such as ravioli or tortellini, whose fillings contrast with its smooth consistency and rich flavor. Be sure to use a fully ripened Haas avocado—the kind with the dark, pebbly skin. It has the best flavor of all avocado varieties.

> ¾ cup heavy cream
> 1 medium Haas avocado, peeled and pitted
> ¾ cup Parmesan cheese
> 2 tablespoons lemon juice
> Salt and freshly ground white pepper

Put the cream in a medium saucepan or skillet over moderate heat.

Meanwhile, in a food processor fitted with the metal blade, puree the avocado with the Parmesan cheese, lemon juice, and salt and pepper.

When the cream is hot but not yet boiling, stir in the avocado mixture. Continue stirring until the sauce is just heated through, 3 to 5 minutes. Pour immediately over cooked pasta.

Serves 4–6

JALAPEÑO CREAM

This is my own version of a sauce created by my friend John Sedlar, owner-chef of Saint Estephe restaurant in Manhattan Beach, California. The hot chili in the sauce gives it a wonderfully delicate, elegant spiciness. (Be careful not to touch your eyes after handling the chilies; wash your hands well.)
Serve with fettuccine, tagliatelli, or other medium ribbons of pasta.

½ **cup white wine vinegar**
½ **teaspoon salt**
1 **medium shallot, finely chopped**
½ **small jalapeño chili, seeded and finely chopped**
3 **cups heavy cream**
2 **tablespoons cilantro leaves, finely chopped (optional)**

Put the vinegar, salt, shallot, and chili in a medium saucepan over moderate-to-high heat. Bring to a boil, then continue boiling briskly until the vinegar has reduced by half, about 5 minutes.

Add the cream and bring it to a full rolling boil. Reduce the heat slightly and gently boil until the sauce reduces by about half to a thick coating consistency, about 20 minutes.

Pour the sauce through a sieve, straining out the shallot and chili pieces. Return the sauce to the pan and gently rewarm it.

Pour over cooked pasta and toss thoroughly. Sprinkle each serving with a little chopped cilantro, if you like.

Serves 4–6

PORCINI-COGNAC CREAM

This is the richest, most seductive cream sauce I know. It's full of the refined yet earthy flavor of dried porcini mushrooms along with an undercurrent of brandy.

Serve over thin-to-medium strands or ribbons of pasta such as angel hair, spaghetti, linguini, or fettuccine.

1½ ounces dried porcini mushrooms
1½ cups cognac or brandy
6 tablespoons unsalted butter
4 large shallots, finely chopped
4 medium garlic cloves, finely chopped
3 cups heavy cream
¾ teaspoon salt
½ teaspoon freshly ground black pepper
3 tablespoons chopped fresh chives

Put the mushrooms in a bowl and add the cognac. Leave them to soak until soft, about 10 minutes. Drain the mushrooms, reserving the cognac, and coarsely chop them.

In a large skillet or saucepan, melt the butter over moderate heat. Add the shallots and garlic; sauté until tender, 2 to 3 minutes. Add the mushrooms and sauté 1 minute more.

Add the reserved cognac to the pan, raise the heat slightly, and simmer for 1 minute. Add the cream and gently boil until the sauce is thick and reduced by half, about 20 minutes more.

Season with salt and black pepper. Pour the sauce over cooked pasta and garnish with chives.

Serves 4-6

5

BUTTER AND OIL SAUCES

OLIVE OIL, HOT CHILIES, AND GARLIC

BROWNED BUTTER, GARLIC, AND PARMESAN

BUTTER, BLACK PEPPER, AND PECORINO

OLIVE OIL, ROMANO, AND GARLIC

BROWNED BREAD CRUMBS, GARLIC, AND PARMESAN

LEMON-HERB BUTTER

BUTTER, SAGE, AND GOAT "PARMESAN"

UMBRIAN AGLIO E OLIO WITH GINGER

BAGNA CAUDA

OLIVE OIL, HOT CHILIES, AND GARLIC

Hot chili peppers and garlic, sizzled until golden in olive oil, meld into a wonderfully rich, complex flavor. If you remove the seeds from the chili pepper, this simple sauce is not too fiery. (Be careful when handling hot chilies that you do not let them touch any cuts in your hands; after handling, take care not to touch your eyes. Severe burning can result. Wash your hands thoroughly with soapy water.)

Serve over spaghetti, linguini, or other medium strands of pasta. Offer plenty of crusty bread to sop the extra oil that sinks to the bottom of the pasta bowls.

1½ cups olive oil
  8 medium garlic cloves, coarsely chopped
  4 green serrano chilies, halved lengthwise, seeded, and sliced thin
  2 red Holland chilies, halved lengthwise, seeded, and thinly sliced
Grated Parmesan cheese

Heat the oil in a large skillet over moderately high heat. Add the garlic and chilies; sauté until golden brown, 2 to 3 minutes. Immediately pour the oil, garlic, and chilies over cooked pasta and toss well. Sprinkle on Parmesan to taste.

Serves 4–6

BROWNED BUTTER, GARLIC, AND PARMESAN

The browned butter in this sauce has a rich, nutty, satisfying flavor that gets extra depth from the Parmesan cheese and garlic it contains. Serve with spaghetti, linguini, or other regular-sized strands, or with filled pastas.

¾ cup (1½ sticks) unsalted butter, cut into pieces
3 medium-to-large garlic cloves, finely chopped
1½ cups grated Parmesan cheese
Salt and freshly ground black pepper

In a medium skillet, melt the butter over moderate heat. When the butter begins to foam, add the garlic, and continue cooking until the butter begins to turn a nut-brown color, about 1 minute more.

Pour the browned garlic butter over cooked pasta, add the Parmesan, and toss well. Season with salt and black pepper to taste.

Serves 4–6

BUTTER, BLACK PEPPER, AND PECORINO

Aged Pecorino is a hard, tangy sheep's milk cheese available in good cheese stores, delis, and Italian markets. It looks like Parmesan cheese but has a much sharper, pleasantly sour flavor.

Black pepper complements it wonderfully. You may even find Pecorino already mixed with cracked black peppercorns.

Serve with spaghetti, fettuccine, or other strands or ribbons of pasta.

1 cup (2 sticks) unsalted butter, cut into pieces
1½ cups grated Pecorino cheese
3 tablespoons coarsely ground black pepper

In a medium skillet, melt the butter over moderate heat. Pour the butter over cooked pasta. Sprinkle on the cheese and black pepper. Toss thoroughly before serving.

Serves 4–6

OLIVE OIL, ROMANO, AND GARLIC

Romano cheese is the Roman version of an aged Pecorino. It has an intensely rich, sharp, yet mellow flavor. If you can't find it, substitute the best Parmesan cheese available. Also in this recipe, use a good virgin olive oil, fruity but not too green.

Serve with spaghetti, linguini, or other regular-sized strands of pasta, or with filled pastas.

¾ cup olive oil
3 medium-to-large garlic cloves, finely chopped
1½ cups grated Romano cheese
Salt and freshly ground black pepper

In a medium skillet, heat the olive oil over moderate heat. Add the garlic and cook until it just begins to turn golden, about 1 minute.

Pour the oil and garlic over cooked pasta, add the Romano, and toss well. Season with salt and black pepper to taste.

Serves 4–6

BROWNED BREAD CRUMBS, GARLIC, AND PARMESAN

This topping is like eating a great garlic-cheese bread and a plate of pasta in one. It's best made with crumbs from a good sourdough loaf.

Serve with spaghetti, linguini, or other medium strands of pasta. It's also good over small macaroni or pasta shells.

- 1½ cups (3 sticks) unsalted butter, cut into pieces
- 1¼ cups fine dry bread crumbs
- 5 medium garlic cloves, finely chopped
- ⅔ cup grated Parmesan cheese
- ¼ cup finely chopped fresh parsley

In a large skillet, melt the butter over moderate heat. As soon as the butter begins to foam, stir in the bread crumbs. Lower the heat slightly and cook them, stirring constantly, until they begin to brown.

Add the garlic and sauté about 1 minute more, until the crumbs are golden-brown. Stir in the Parmesan and parsley. Pour immediately over cooked pasta. Toss well before serving.

Serves 4–6

LEMON-HERB BUTTER

Fresh herbs are a must for this light springtime sauce. Serve it with delicate pasta strands, such as angel hair, or use it to coat filled pastas.

¾ cup (1½ sticks) unsalted butter, cut into pieces
6 tablespoons lemon juice
1 tablespoon chopped fresh parsley
1 tablespoon chopped fresh chives
1½ teaspoons chopped fresh dill
1½ teaspoons chopped fresh tarragon leaves
Salt
Freshly ground white pepper

In a medium saucepan or skillet, melt the butter with the lemon juice over moderate heat. As soon as the butter has melted completely, stir in the herbs. Season with salt and white pepper to taste. Pour over the cooked pasta.

Serves 4–6

BUTTER, SAGE, AND GOAT "PARMESAN"

Many gourmet markets now carry grated, dried, domestic goat's milk cheese that's a lot like Parmesan cheese. It has the rich, slightly sour tang of a good goat cheese, combined with the mellowness that comes from age.

In this dish, the sweet, spicy flavor of fresh sage provides a wonderful contrast to the cheese. If you can't find such a cheese, substitute Pecorino or the tangiest Parmesan cheese you can find.

Serve over spaghetti, linguini, or other medium strands of pasta. It also goes well with small macaroni or pasta shells.

1½ **cups (3 sticks) unsalted butter, cut into pieces**
2½ **tablespoons chopped fresh sage leaves**
  1 **cup grated aged goat cheese**

In a large skillet, melt the butter over moderate heat. Immediately add the sage leaves and sauté them for about 1 minute.

Pour the butter and sage over cooked pasta. Sprinkle on the goat cheese and toss well before serving.

Serves 4–6

UMBRIAN AGLIO E OLIO WITH GINGER

In the Umbrian region of central Italy, fresh ginger is a popular seasoning. Here it adds extra spark to a simple, traditional sauce of virgin olive oil and garlic. Serve over angel hair, spaghettini, or other delicate strands of pasta.

1½ cups olive oil
10 medium garlic cloves, coarsely chopped
3 tablespoons finely chopped fresh ginger
Grated Parmesan cheese

Heat the oil in a large skillet over moderately high heat. Add the garlic and ginger; sauté until golden brown, 2 to 3 minutes.

Immediately pour the oil, garlic, and ginger over cooked pasta and toss well. Sprinkle on Parmesan to taste.

Serves 4-6

BAGNA CAUDA

This "hot bath" of olive oil, butter, garlic, anchovies, and white truffles is traditionally served as a dip for raw vegetables, crusty bread, or bread sticks in the Piedmont region of northwestern Italy. Here, it makes a spectacular sauce for pasta.

Instead of going to the expense and trouble of purchasing white truffles, I use white truffle-scented olive oil. Small bottles of it are available at gourmet stores where the price is relatively low compared to the price of truffles themselves (though this scented oil still is costlier than plain olive oil).

Serve over spaghetti, linguini, fettuccine, or other medium strands or medium ribbons of pasta. Be sure to serve lots of bread for sopping extra sauce.

- 1 **cup (2 sticks) unsalted butter, cut into pieces**
- ½ **cup white truffle-scented olive oil**
- 6 **medium garlic cloves, finely chopped**
- 2 **2-ounce tins anchovy fillets, drained and chopped fine**

In a medium saucepan, melt the butter with the scented oil and garlic over very low heat. As soon as the butter has melted, stir in the anchovy fillets. Continue stirring until they've dissolved. Pour over cooked pasta and toss well.

Serves 4–6

INDEX